On Writing for Children and Other Peopl
808 LES

Lester. Juliu

D0594226

DATE DUE

ON *Writing*
FOR
CHILDREN
&
OTHER
PEOPLE

JULIUS LESTER

ON *Writing*

FOR

CHILDREN

&

OTHER

PEOPLE

Dial Books — *New York*

Published by Dial Books
A member of Penguin Group (USA) Inc.
345 Hudson Street
New York, New York 10014

Copyright © 2004 by Julius Lester
Designed by Nancy R. Leo-Kelly
Text set in Zapf Rennaissance
Printed in the U.S.A. on acid-free paper
1 2 3 4 5 6 7 8 9 10

Library of Congress Cataloging-in-Publication Data
Lester, Julius.
On writing for children and other people / Julius Lester.
p.   cm.
ISBN 0-8037-2867-0
1. Lester, Julius. 2. Authors, American—20th century—Biography.
3. Children's literature—Authorship. 4. Lester, Julius—Authorship.
5. Authorship. I. Title.
PS3562.E853Z468 2004   813'.54—dc22   2003027090

Portions of this manuscript appeared in
The Horn Book, The New Advocate, Riverbank Review,
and *Storytelling Magazine* in radically differently form.

All photos by Julius Lester except: *pg. 18,* Rev. W. D. Lester Sr.;
pg. 38 top, Dorothy Green; *pg. 38 bottom,* unknown; *pg. 46,* unknown.

For Phyllis Fogelman and Neil Ross,
who make a difference

And for my wife, Milan,
who is the difference

Mississippi, 1966

By Way of Introduction

For the past forty-seven years I have devoted most of my time and energy to writing. For the most part I cannot say I have enjoyed it. Writing has been a vocation in the original sense of the word, that is a religious calling, one I was helpless to deny.

In the last year or so I have sensed that, at long last, the strength of that call is beginning to wane. While I probably will never stop writing entirely, the compulsion and need to write no longer sits at the core of my being burning like a prairie wildfire one watches, helpless to do anything but wait until the flames have nothing else on which to feed.

My energy is beginning to turning inward. For me at age sixty-five, this is appropriate as circumstances are requiring that I begin making peace with my mortality. A series of events have compelled me to recognize that this is the direction my vocation must now take.

In the fall of 1998 my wife and I were driving back to our home in western Massachusetts from St. Johnsbury,

Vermont, where I had been lay leader of Beth El Synagogue since 1992. On that drive I became aware of a hissing noise in my ears, a sound that combined the chirping of crickets with the white noise of a radio or television set. I had always had problems on airplanes with my ears stopping up and I assumed the hissing noise was a new variant of my reaction to altitude. But the hissing continued even after we returned to the lower altitude of where we lived. Days passed. The noise remained with me like a dog that follows you home and sits on the porch, waiting, as if he is going to belong to you whether you want him or not. I wondered if the hissing was the onset of deafness, a condition I fully expected to have since it characterized the last years of my grandmother, my mother, and her three siblings.

My doctor sent me to a hearing specialist and a series of tests revealed that, yes, I was beginning to lose some hearing in the highest frequencies but that was normal at fifty-nine, my age then. The hissing noise I was hearing, however, was tinnitus. No one knew what caused it and there was no cure, the doctor told me blithely, and sent me back to my primary care physician. He told me, "There's nothing I can do. You have to learn to live with it." He had no suggestions as to how I was supposed to do this, or showed any interest in helping me find out. I decided that the first step in learning to live with tinnitus was to find a sympathetic doctor.

As my children will tell you, my sensitivity to noise was responsible for repressing much of the spontaneity of their childhoods. I thought my fanatical need for silence was a personal quirk until I learned of a condition called hyperacusis, abnormal sensitivity to sound. It seemed cruel that someone who loved and needed silence as much as I did should have to live with a constant hissing that sometimes escalated into a loud ringing. In 1996 my wife and I bought a house and twelve acres that were hidden from the road by trees and where the silence is broken more often by the cawing of crows, the whelps of young foxes, and the rustling of dead leaves as wild turkeys make their way slowly out of the woods. Silence had become my worst enemy. I needed to be living in New York, where I might not have noticed even that I had tinnitus.

I refused to accept that there was no cure or, at least, relief. A search on the World Wide Web brought me to the site of the American Tinnitus Association, which I joined, and through its publications and my own research I learned that tinnitus might not be a disorder of the inner ear. It was posssible that the brain was misinterpreting information it received from the ears. There was no hissing sound to be heard. The brain only *thought* there was, which was why one could be deaf and still have tinnitus.

Nonetheless, I tried acupuncture and cranio-sacral therapy, but neither brought any relief. I learned to carry earplugs at all times and wore them in movie theaters, where the volume of sound tracks is often at dangerous levels. I had to put my fingers in my ears against the sirens of fire trucks and police cars, which could turn a mild hissing sound into loud ringing. At home I listened to music to mask the sound but there were times, like now as I write, that the hissing is so loud I can scarcely hear the music.

After a year or so the sounds ceased to draw my attention as much as they had at the beginning, and many days the hissing is at a level low enough that I am able to ignore it. Sometimes I am even able to focus my attention on the silence and hear it instead of the hissing. Through *Tinnitus Today*, the journal of the American Tinnitus Association, I learned that some people had had success in controlling tinnitus with Elavil, a mild tranquilizer. My new doctor's research confirmed this and he wrote me a prescription. I now have weeks, instead of hours or days, in which there is no hissing.

During that first year of learning to live with tinnitus, I happened to be reading to my wife from the selected letters of Carl Jung. In one he acknowledged his own tinnitus. He interpreted the noises as an effort by the unconscious "to make psychic contents audible" and force one's "attention inwards, where of course it gets caught in the disturbing noises."

> I know from experience that the demand of the unconscious for introversion—in your case the ability to listen inwards—is unusually great. And equally great is the danger that instead of *being able* to listen inwards one is *compelled* to listen inwards. (C. G. Jung Letters. Vol. 2, 1951–1961, p. 20)

Jung's words affirmed the sense that both my wife and I had that there was something within I was supposed to be listening to. Listening is a complex endeavor, which is why I find it significant that one of the central prayers of

Judaism is an exhortation to listen: "Sh'ma Yisrael Adonai Eloheinu Adonai Echad—Hear O Israel: The Lord our God, The Lord is One." Throughout my life I had taken pride in how well I listened to the vibrations and echoes of feelings that lay deep within. However, if Jung's analysis was correct, and I thought it was, the tinnitus indicated I had not been listening very well at all, or that there was something new trying to get my attention.

There was no epiphany. Revelation came gradually, imperceptibly. I learned that I was tired of some aspects of the life I had created for myself. Twenty to thirty weeks of the past fifteen to twenty years I had been on airplanes going to give lectures at colleges and universities, synagogues, and Jewish community centers about my conversion to Judaism and on black and Jewish relations. Some months I slept more nights in hotel and motel beds than in my own. I had begun to fear that I would die in a hotel room and the last sound I would hear would be the ice machine in the hall next to my room, a room I often seemed to be given, grinding out another load of cubes. I recalled that Don Drysdale, the great pitcher for the Dodgers, had been found dead of a heart attack in a hotel room by a maid who deserved a better start to her day.

I was even more weary, however, of appearing in public, and the positive and negative attributes that were projected onto me. I was not mired in "racial self-hatred," as many blacks thought, nor was I the "inspiration" many Jews saw me as. I was me, a person more complex (and, my wife maintains, simpler) than any of the labels attached to my name—black, Jew, children's book author, professor. I began saying no to some lecture invitations, but I was not yet ready to end what had become a way of life.

Two years after the onset of tinnitus, my wife and I were again in St. Johnsbury. It was going to be a busy weekend because in addition to conducting Friday night and Saturday morning services, I was also going to meet with a couple at whose wedding I would be co-officiating with a rabbi, and I had to be at the mikvah—ritual bath—in Burlington on Sunday for the conversion ceremony of a congregant and her two sons.

As I started to get out of the motel bed that Saturday morning, the room began spinning in circles of such violence that I felt sick to my stomach and found myself unable to stand or even sit. I knew immediately what was happening. I'd had intermittent vertigo spells for almost twenty years, but none as severe as the one that Shabbat morning. I lay in bed and even the simplest motion to sit up caused me to scream and cry. My body seemed as if it were no longer contained by gravity. I had no physical substance except when lying down and staring straight up because the slightest movement of my head made me cry out.

Any traveler's nightmare is becoming seriously ill in a strange town. But there is probably no synagogue in America that does not have at least one doctor among its members. Little Beth El Synagogue in St. Johnsbury, Vermont, with a membership of sixty families and single people, was no exception. Dr. Will Birge had tried to help me with the tinnitus as a concerned friend, so my wife called him and we drove to his office in St. Albans,

Vermont, on the Canadian border. His diagnosis was Ménière's disease, which people with tinnitus were susceptible to. He gave me Meclazine for the dizziness, and Valium, and when I asked whether I would be well enough to meet with the couple and be present for the conversion, he told my wife to take me home.

My previous vertigo attacks had involved little more than a slight loss of balance, which caused me to walk as if I were drunk, and they never lasted more than a day or two. The effects of the attack that Shabbat morning lasted almost two weeks. There was also the added anxiety of not knowing if the vertigo would be permanent, which is always a possibility. I've only had one attack as severe since and this one was shorter in duration.

With the unpredictability of vertigo it was clear I could no longer travel alone. I retired from the lecture circuit and in the fall of 2001 I stopped going to Beth El one weekend each month and now go only to lead Rosh Hashanah and Yom Kippur services.

However, there was another health issue to contend with, one far more serious than tinnitus or vertigo. In 2000 I was diagnosed with asthma and emphysema. I had stopped smoking in 1988 (July 13, 2:45 P.M.), but not soon enough to prevent irreversible damage to my lungs. Knowing nothing about the disease, my first reaction was that it was a death sentence. But emphysema is not a terminal illness; it is a chronic condition. While there is no cure, or drugs designed specifically for it, regular exercise helps the body utilize more efficiently what oxygen the lungs can make available.

Tinnitus. Vertigo. Emphysema. Each one seemed to be telling me I was supposed to stay at home, which I was doing, and happily. I thought I had done well at inner listening and had made the changes the unconscious required. Perhaps, but apparently there was another change I needed to make.

On July 13, 2001, I was traveling south on West Street in Hadley, Massachusetts. A truck was standing at the stop sign where Cemetery Road crosses West. As I approached the intersection I saw the truck suddenly leap forward as the driver hit the accelerator. I swerved my car but knew I was going to be hit. I relaxed my body and the instant before impact I said to myself: *Am I going to die? What a stupid way to die.*

The emergency room doctor thought I only had bruised ribs and I was released the same day. But as the days passed the pain only intensified and it became increasingly difficult to breathe. Because of the emphysema, I had purchased an oximeter so I could measure the oxygen saturation in my blood when I exercised. Four days after the accident my breathing had become so labored it was difficult to talk. The oximeter told me why. My oxygen saturation had dropped to eighty-two. In a person with healthy lungs, normal is ninety-six to one hundred. My norm was ninety-three. A visit to my doctor and a call to my pulmonologist finally determined that the emergency room doctor had misread my X rays. Instead of bruised ribs I had two broken ribs, a broken collar bone, and a collapsed left lung.

I was in the hospital for five days before the lung reinflated sufficiently for me to be released, but I would be on oxygen for a month. The physical recovery from the accident was two months of the most excruciating pain, including days of suicidal depression and insomnia as I underwent withdrawal from the pain killer Oxycontin. Psychological recovery took far longer, and I still have moments when I replay the accident, and while driving I still flinch when I see a car or truck waiting at a stop sign to cross an intersection.

There was still something the unconscious was asking of me, something I was either unable to hear or refusing to. I had stopped traveling and lecturing and leading services. Nothing remained except teaching and writing. But the imperatives of spiritual development require us to give close attention to the needs of the soul, which are, all too often, ignored for the more immediate desires of the ego.

Again, there was no epiphany. Instead, I began to wonder if I was tired of writing. In 1979 I had a dream in which a voice said, "Each writing is an act of faith that requires the strength of ten thousand men." Slowly, it became apparent: I don't have that faith or strength any longer. Maybe I merely need a respite. But maybe I am truly done with writing. For years I have told friends that one day I would enter silence. But with my brain hearing a sound that does not exist, that may no longer be possible. But that's all right. More recently I've been telling friends I want to learn to see. To do that I must learn not to listen to the mind's incessant chatter and look, for example, at a plant without classifying it, without even wanting to know its name (as if plants know they have names). To see means to look at the color of a plant's leaves and flowers without naming them. To see is to do as Blake admonished and "cleanse the doors of perception." Perhaps learning to see is another way of entering the silence.

As I contemplate the closure of my life as a writer, I have never been happier. I cannot imagine what my life would be like if I did not have tinnitus, vertigo, and emphysema, if I had not had the accident. Some days, weeks, and even months life is difficult physically, but I do not want any other life than this one. I am grateful to tinnitus, vertigo, and especially emphysema for what they offer my humanity.

As I come to what may be the end of my writing life, I need to know how and why I became a writer, especially because music and art have been at least as important to me, if not more so. I have always been frustrated that writing exists in only one dimension. When I used to play piano, and now when I listen to music, I love the interplay of sound in the lines of a Bach fugue. In art and photography I love how light, color, form, and composition create a multitextured whole. But each art form has its limitations. Music is bound in time, existing only as one note fades and another begins. Painting and photography are confined by the shape of the canvas, the boundaries of a single frame of film. Perhaps in an attempt to overcome the inherent limitation of every art form, words have been set to music, music to motion pictures, and photographs are often accompanied by words. As humans we want to express as much as is in us and no single art form is sufficient to the enormity of the task.

So, this book has three dimensions. The first is the text itself, the theme at the center of contrapuntal lines. The second is the quotations that begin each section. Most are from writers who write for children—and other people. My work does not exist in isolation but is part of a continuum comprised of men and women for whom it is a sacred task to offer to children books that care about story and language.

The third dimension is the images, primarily of children into whose faces I have gazed, faces that have probed mine with far more intensity than any adult would dare. Many writers do not think about readers as they write. They say to do so would distract them from the stories they are trying to tell. Perhaps because I was born black at a certain time and place in American history, I cannot write without conscious awareness that for me "writing is a social act," as my friend, writer Shulamith Oppenheim told me once, quoting something she heard Albert Einstein say. Even though I am alone as I write and you are alone as you read, we are joined by a desire, a need to know something about who we are and why we are here. That need dominated my childhood and remains central to my life even now.

As you read I would like you to take time to look at the images. They are the text also. For me writing has never been about self-expression. I have my journal for that. Writing has been about tending the spirit and making real the soul. Look into these souls. Perhaps you will see your own.

Julius Lester at three years old, 1942

We spend our years as a tale that is told.

Psalms 90:9

I was never a child. My parents were in their forties when I was born. Not having had childhoods of their own, they did not know how to give me one. Both of my father's parents died before he was fifteen, leaving him to raise his two younger brothers alone. My mother's father died before she was old enough to remember what he looked like, leaving her mother alone to raise four children at a time when single mothers were rare.

Childhood was a luxury my parents could not afford, nor one they could afford for me because of racial segregation and its attendant psychic violence. In their childhoods and mine black males were lynched if they even looked like they were thinking of threatening the social order.

My father's profession also contributed to my being denied a childhood. He was a Methodist minister who believed it was a sin to go to the movies on Sundays, play marbles for "keeps" (that was gambling), play cards, listen to secular music, dance, and for women to wear pants or smoke. As my father was God's representative, I, his second and last child and youngest son, was expected to be God's ambassador, also. Perhaps because my mother had to live with the expectations projected onto her as the wife of a minister, she understood that such expectations might be too burdensome for a child, and when Daddy left the house to do errands or went on trips, she let me listen to the radio and occasionally she and I even played cards. Outside the house, however, I was a spiritual extension of my father, "Julius, Reb'n Lester's son." Not only could I not do anything that might even remotely be considered "bad," I was also given responsibilities other boys were not.

In kindergarten the teacher assigned me to sit with a boy who was mentally retarded and asked me to help him with lessons and be his friend. (There was no such thing as "special ed" in 1945.) I don't recall how I felt about having someone put into my care. However, there must have been some resentment because one day William, I'll call him, reached beneath the table at which we were sitting and hit me on the leg, hard. (I have no doubt I said or did something to provoke him.) I forgot I was God's envoy and keeper of my father's good name and hit him back and didn't bother to do it under the table. The teacher called me to the front of the class and spanked me. When she finished I didn't give her the satisfaction of crying and instead told her angrily, "He hit me first!" She surprised me when she said, "I know. I saw him." Before I could ask her to explain the unjust punishment she had just rendered to my behind, she said, "You're Reverend Lester's son. You know better."

I submitted to the truth of her words. She was right. I *was* Reverend Lester's son and, indeed, I did know better. Perhaps I would not have so readily accepted that identity if not for my brother. Sonny was nine years my senior and he worked diligently to commit almost every sin our father preached against. Sonny gambled, partied hard, and one unforgettable Sunday morning he came to church straight from a party reeking of alcohol. Daddy stopped preaching in midsermon and was taking off his belt as he came down from the pulpit. He grabbed my brother from the pew where he sat next to me and Mother and proceeded to beat him with the belt. When he finished, he put his belt back on, returned to the pulpit, and resumed preaching as if nothing had happened. If a minister couldn't control his own children, how could he expect a congregation to follow him? Daddy certainly gained the congregation's respect that Sunday morning, but he also lost his firstborn son, who left home to join the Coast Guard when he was seventeen and never grew beyond his anger at our father (nor his anger at me for being raised by a father who learned to leaven his strictness with love. By the time I reached adolescence he let me listen to the radio and paid for my considerable jazz collection).

I was only eight when my brother left home in 1947. I saw him fewer than ten times between then and his death in 1989, five months before his sixtieth birthday. I sat by his bed in the hospital room for three days during the last month of his life. We had nothing to say to each other.

Sonny was a major influence in my life as my father held him before my eyes in the words of an oft-repeated mantra: "Don't be like your brother. You're going to be *someBODY!*"

The last sentence was heard by many black sons in the 1940s. "You're going to be *someBODY!*" our parents and teachers told us, infusing those two syllables with the anguished dreams of every black man and woman since the first African stepped off the slave ship *Jesus* in the colony of Virginia in 1619. We didn't need to be told what being *someBODY* meant. Even in the womb we had overheard our parents and other adults talking about *white folks* and all they did "to keep the Negro down."

We traveled a lot during the summers, and whenever my father had to get gas, I watched tensely from the backseat as the white station attendant came to the car. If he said, "What can I get for you, boy?" I knew my father would respond, "Not a damn thing, Sam," one of the few times I ever heard him use a curse word, and speed away from the station, tires squealing. Daddy didn't expect a white person to address him as "sir," but he would not tolerate being addressed as "boy."

In 1945 we drove to California from Kansas City, Kansas, where we'd lived since I was two. We stopped in Denver, Colorado, to visit friends for a few days before continuing on to San Francisco, our ultimate destination. In those days when blacks traveled they took as much food with them as they could because they could not be assured of finding a public place at which to eat, even in the North. There was the additional problem of somewhere to stay. We didn't know anyone between Denver and San Francisco and even if there'd been motels then, they, like the hotels, would have been closed to blacks.

That trip gave me my first opportunity to practice what being someBODY meant. The food our friends in Denver had prepared for us had been eaten and digested for some time when we reached Carson City, Nevada. Daddy drove slowly along the main street looking for someplace where we might go in and eat. Some cafés had signs on the doors or in the windows— NO COLORED ALLOWED—while others *looked* like they had signs. Finally Daddy parked in front of a restaurant without a sign and whose brightly lit interior made it appear "friendly." He went inside.

Scarcely a minute passed before he returned to the car. "I asked the peckerwood if we could come in and sit down and eat. He said we could buy something and take it out. He said he was sorry and he seemed like he was embarrassed a little." Even though I was only six, Daddy didn't have to explain. If we couldn't sit down and eat like everybody else, we weren't going to buy food and eat in the car.

I don't remember if we eventually found somewhere to eat. I don't remember if I was hungry. All I remember is that physical discomfort was nothing compared to living with the memory of spiritual humiliation. Whatever else being *someBODY* might mean, it meant not cooperating with the white world's efforts to demean us.

There was no time nor space in those years for what we now think of as childhood—an expanse of years in which one is protected from the outside world and the primary activity is play. Yes, I played games (though primarily with girls. Boys wrestled and did other things that could get you hurt. Nobody ever scraped a knee or broke a bone playing with dolls, and yes, I had my own doll). Play was a diversion that had no connection to becoming the *someBODY* my people needed me to be.

Having to carry the promise of a people's unfulfilled dreams increased and intensified the fear that permeates childhood normally. Many people romanticize childhood as Edenic, and maybe it is for some. For others of us, though, childhood is veined with anxiety created by our physical and emotional dependence on adults whose moods can be as capricious as a tornado that levels the houses on only one side of a street. Maybe some of us write for children because our emotions remember that childhood is a stressful and fearful time, because one is small and everyone and everything else is enormous and you can be swallowed whole without warning.

I was four or five and was with my parents in Kansas City, Missouri, the larger and more metropolitan city across the viaduct from Kansas City, Kansas, as they did their Christmas shopping. Even now, some sixty years later, I feel the terror that rose within me when one second I was holding my father's hand, and the next second that hand was gone. The street corner swarms with people but I am too small to see faces. There is only a blue, black, and brown maelstrom of winter coats. A scream of such desperate panic tears from my throat that all the blue, black, and brown coats rushing past stop. And then, there is my father's familiar hand grasping mine. He had only loosed my hand to button his coat but, surrounded by the crowds of holiday shoppers, I had been unable to see enough of him to recognize that of all the adults, he was the one who belonged to me.

Childhood is also a time of fear because our minds do not have the language and concepts to make sense of what we see and hear. We depend on adults to give us the language that will create order and protect us from chaos. But what words can black parents use to make sense of racism for their children?

Wisely, the adults of my childhood years didn't try to explain why white people treated us as if we were incapable of feeling pain. Neither did they hide their contempt for whites and in casual conversations referred to them as "peckerwoods," "crackers," and "white trash." Once a white insurance salesman came to the door of our house, and from my hiding place behind my mother's skirts, I poked my head out and yelled, "Woodpecker!" deliberately reversing the syllables so I could express the same disdain I'd heard from my parents but not get in trouble for saying what I knew to be a "bad word."

We survived segregation with a modicum of self-respect by not cooperating with the system unless there was no alternative. I walked almost everywhere so as not to ride the segregated buses. The law required blacks to sit in the back and, if the bus filled, to get up and give our seats to whites. I did not go to white movie theaters because I would have had to sit in the balcony. Except for Miss Nye, a white piano teacher I had in early childhood who introduced me to the music of Johann Sebastian Bach, I cannot recall speaking to a white person until we moved to Nashville, Tennessee, when I was fourteen. (Because my father traveled a lot to conduct revivals, he could not control his contact with whites. He would tell us about riding in segregated railroad cars and having a screen placed around his table when he went to the dining car to eat so whites wouldn't have to see him.)

Race was complicated for me, however, because I was not always sure who was and who wasn't white. My father was very dark-skinned and was obviously "colored," as we called ourselves then, but my mother's complexion was very light and she had long, almost straight black hair. More than once my father came close to being arrested by white policemen who stopped his car thinking he was with a white woman. My grandmother and two of her children were light-skinned enough to pass for white and did on occasion, especially when they had to see a doctor.

Given that my family came in all shades, from

white like my grandmother, mother, and an aunt and an uncle to black like my father, I wasn't sure I knew what white people looked like. But I kept my ignorance to myself, not wanting my parents to know how dumb I was.

I was in third grade and the burden of my racial ignorance had become more than I could bear. I must have liked and trusted my third-grade teacher very much because one day in class she asked if we had any questions. My hand shot up.

"What do white people look like?" I asked when she called on me.

My classmates almost died premature deaths from laughing so hard. Fortunately the teacher knew my family and understood why I needed to ask.

"White people have big noses," she said very seriously.

Thus a measure of order and intelligibility was brought to my personal world where people looked white but weren't. (I did wonder if the white doctors who treated my aunt and uncle might notice their small noses and throw them out for not being truly white.) However, if I could now distinguish visually between whites and blacks, I still had to decipher the language of a world in which everything was defined by race.

Every summer until I was fourteen my mother

took me to visit her mother, who lived outside Pine Bluff, Arkansas. I was perhaps six the day Mother and I were in a store downtown. It was hot in the store because if air-conditioning had been invented by the late 1940s, it hadn't made its way to the Arkansas delta. In a corner of the store I saw two water fountains. One was tall and above it was a sign that read WHITE. Next to it at what was the perfect height for a child was another fountain. Above it the sign read COLORED. WHITE water didn't sound very appealing, but I imagined COLORED water would be as beautiful as Joseph's coat. I went over to the COLORED water fountain, but just as I got there my mother's hand gently grabbed my shoulder.

"You can't drink out of there," she said.

I didn't ask why because something in her voice conveyed that this "colored" was not a rainbow-sparkling spray. No. This was COLORED like the sign on the bus we had to take to and from town because Grandmother lived too far away from town for us to walk. This COLORED was like the COLORED signs at the bus and train stations indicating what doors COLORED PEOPLE could use and at which windows they could buy tickets. That was not colored water. It was COLORED water and I think my mother would have watched me die of thirst before she let me drink from a COLORED fountain.

The acquisition of language gives a child a degree of safety in and control over his world. Again, it was a summer in Pine Bluff. I was reading the newspaper and came across an article about a "colored boy" who had been arrested for the rape of a white woman. I was an excellent reader and I knew how to pronounce the word *rape*, but I didn't know what it meant. However, because it was used in conjunction with something done to a white woman by a colored man, I knew whatever he'd done wasn't good. Blacks were not mentioned in southern newspapers of the time unless they had committed a crime.

"What does rap mean?" I asked my mother, deliberately mispronouncing the word.

"What're you reading?" she demanded in that annoyed tone she used when I wanted to know something she didn't want to tell me. I handed her the newspaper and pointed to the article.

"Rape," she said, pronouncing the word correctly She handed the paper back to me and walked away, probably troubled that she didn't know how to explain it to an eight-year-old, as troubled as I would have been trying to understand.

Language was also an arena in which subtle and deadly serious jousting with whites occurred, as I learned after we moved to Nashville. An unwritten southern law was that blacks had to address whites as "sir," and "ma'am." However, if you were a black in training to be *someBODY*, you said "sir" or "ma'am" to a white person only if you were in danger of being beaten or killed, and blacks had been lynched for failing to address white men as "sir." Having observed how my father avoided saying "sir" and "ma'am" to white people, I knew the art of survival lay in one's tone of voice and choice of words. A typical scene would go something like this:

I approach the checkout counter in a store.

WHITE CLERK [whose southern accent evokes images of lynchings in ME]: "Is that all?"

ME [knowing I am supposed to answer "Yassuh" with a pleasant smile]: "Yes, I believe it is."

WHITE CLERK [gives ME a sharp look, knowing he is being insulted but can't figure out how. CLERK decides to try again]: "You sure there ain't nothing else you need?"

ME [careful not to look WHITE CLERK in eyes and be accused of being "an uppity nigger," say politely]: "Thank you, but there's nothing else."

Often clerks would persist in trying to make me say "sir" or "ma'am," but I never did. Once, however, as I was leaving a store the clerk said ominously, "You better learn some manners, boy." I didn't learn any "manners," nor did I ever go back to that store.

The pervasive assault of racism and the terrorism inherent in racial segregation were counterbalanced by a community that gave my life focus and purpose because it had chosen me to be *someBODY*, to slay the white dragon through the sheer power of intellectual accomplishments. The books I read reflected the archetypal drama for which I was being prepared. There were countless ones of history and biography and though I do not remember a single event or person about whom I read, I knew even then that I was seeking answers to some of the central questions of my life: Why do things happen the way they do? How do you create a life despite adversity?

Those books did not provide me with answers but something far more important: the presences of people who, merely through using words, reached out to me across the vastness. The word *book* comes from a root meaning "beech tree." I imagine a beech staff standing in a forest clearing, runes inscribed on it. It does not matter what the runes represented. What matters is that one person was attempting to reach out to others whom he or she may not have known. The mystery and miracle of a book lies in its embodiment of a solitary voice penetrating time and space to go beyond time and space and alight for a moment in that place within each of us that is also beyond time and space.

Books gave me the emotional knowledge that the world in which I was forced to live bounded by the white heat of hatred was not the only reality. Books introduced me to the power of dreams and that sometimes the courage to dream was more important than the content of the dream.

But there was another dimension to my reading, one that had potentially disturbing consequences. I can't recall how I started reading pulp magazines in which article after article recounted true stories of gruesome murders. *Police Gazette, True Crime,* and similar magazines carried crime scene photographs of bloody murder victims lying in ditches, in the street, or on the floor of their houses. I loved these magazines, their stories and photographs. I was eight years old.

I also read comic books by the hundreds, especially those featuring superheroes like Superman and Batman, as well as horror comics. Such reading fare, with its emphasis on bloody and gory deaths, reflected the world in which I was growing up far better and more accurately than the children's books of the times.

I read the traditional fairy tales, but I seemed to miss the "point." In "Jack and the Beanstalk," I rooted for the giant; in "Little Red Riding Hood" and "The Three Little Pigs," I was definitely cheering for the wolf. I liked that the ogres and villains of horror comics often emerged triumphant and that some murderers were never caught.

I am grateful my parents never questioned or

derided what I read. Maybe they understood on some primal level what I was doing, though I was far into adulthood before I did. By reading pulp magazines and comics I was trying to neutralize the violence intrinsic to my dailiness. In reading about violence I isolated and objectified it. Violence was not unique to my neighborhood, I learned, and it was especially reassuring to read that white people were victims of brutal violence, too. My parents left me alone to read what I wanted to, trusting me to care for my soul, though I did not know consciously that was what I was doing.

Caring for the soul is an intricate and lifelong process. That process is illuminated and made easier by the quality of language we are able to bring to it. Aldous Huxley wrote: "Words have power to mould men's thinking, to canalize their feeling, to direct their willing and acting. *Conduct and character are largely determined by the nature of the words we currently use to discuss ourselves and the world around us.*" (Italics added.)

In my father's preaching, and that of other black ministers, I experienced language as a power that brought forth tears and shouts of joy from congregations of hundreds. I learned that language was not only words and their meanings but that music and rhythm were part of the meaning. My father was the conductor of an orchestra of emotions and on Sunday mornings he exorcized pain, frustration, hardship from the souls of the congregation and replaced them with joy and hope and the promise of ultimate salvation. And he did it with words.

There was also the language of story and I loved it when my father was with a group of ministers and they started telling tales about Brer Rabbit, why black people had to work so hard, and how the ol' slave John tricked the slave master. Words had the power to make people laugh, and I experienced that power when I found a joke or story my father had not heard (or at least one he pretended he hadn't) and made him laugh. How incredible that something I *said* could evoke joy.

But words had another dimension and power, one more mysterious than that I experienced in my father's preaching. I want you to imagine the front porch of an unpainted house on a wide expanse of land outside Pine Bluff, Arkansas. It is a time when the poles and wires that bring electricity to the homes of whites have not been extended to blacks. (When it finally was, my grandmother refused it, saying, "I don't want no fire running through my house." Ironically, shortly before her death in 1965 her house was destroyed by fire and she barely escaped.) I want you to imagine the darkness of nights that have never been diluted by the luminescence of bulbs. This is a darkness not threatened by the feeble light given off by the coal oil lamps I see in the windows of houses scattered over the countryside. This is a darkness so thick that though I am sitting next to my mother in the wooden swing suspended by two chains from hooks in the porch ceiling, I cannot see her. Nor can I see my grandmother on the other side of the porch, where she sits near her brother, my great-uncle Rudolph. Then, suddenly, into this darkness comes my grandmother's gruff voice:

"Beatrice?" she calls out, addressing my mother by her middle name. "Do you remember Ruth Williams?"

There is silence and though I cannot see her I can visualize my mother going into her memory like someone walking through thick underbrush, pushing branches to the side and creating a trail where none exists. Finally, Mother says, "Did she have a brother, a tall, ugly boy, believe his name was Gerald?"

"That's her!" Grandmother says immediately, delighted that she and her oldest daughter have met in the intimacy of memory. "Well, let me tell you what happened to her."

My grandmother would proceed to relate the woes that had befallen Ruth Williams (though she didn't know what had happened to her tall, ugly brother but she thought she'd heard he was in "the pen"). I would listen intently, trying to imagine what Ruth

Williams looked like and how it felt to be her when fate unfolded and crushed her as if she were nothing more than a mosquito slapped into a quick death for whining too close to someone's ear.

There was something primeval about those evenings sitting on the porch in the dark at my grandmother's. Most of the stories told throughout human history have been spoken into the darkness, or around a fire with a vast, impenetrable darkness surrounding teller and listeners. When one barely sees the storyteller and the expressions crossing his face, the voice and the words become living entities in the mysterious and fearful darkness, joining listener to listener and listeners to speaker. In his story the teller retrieves from death the souls of whom he speaks. I had never known Ruth Williams but my grandmother and my mother brought her into my life and, almost sixty years after that night on my grandmother's porch, to this page.

My grandmother Emma Altschul Smith

My mother, Julia Beatrice Smith Lester

I haven't really written my plays and books—I've heard them. The stories are there already, singing in your genes and in your blood.

Sebastian Barry

Hearing the voices of my mother and grandmother coming out of the darkness was one of my introductions to the imagination, a faculty as vital to our lives as reason, perhaps more so. The root meaning of imagine is "to picture to oneself." This is different from the memories we have of people and events we have experienced directly. My mother and grandmother remembered Ruth Williams. I had to imagine her. The realm of memory is finite. That of the imagination is infinite because it enables us to see what we have not seen, what we may never see, what may not even exist. Imagination enables us to experience what it is like to be someone else.

My father wanted me to know what it had been like to be him and he told me stories of his life in the South during those decades when, in the words of James Weldon Johnson, "hope unborn had died." In

39

listening to his stories, I learned that I came from a people who had been thrown into a fiery furnace and had not been consumed. I learned that I, too, could withstand the heat and the flames and walk out of the furnace, strutting.

My seventh-grade homeroom teacher, Rozetta K. Caldwell, introduced me to another dimension of story and expanded my experience with the imagination. She taught history but not only from books. She told us about the native Americans who had lived in places we passed every day on our walks to and from school. Behind what our eyes saw there was another time and other people. Because of Miss Caldwell I stopped seeing only what was before my eyes and began trying to see what had been. Whenever my parents drove across the viaduct that connected Kansas City, Kansas, and Kansas City, Missouri, I tried not to see the meat-packing plant and airport bordering the place where the Kaw River joined the Missouri, but trees and Indians in canoes.

Next to the public library in Kansas City, Kansas, is a burial ground of the Kaw Indians. I remember walking along the broad walkway to the library and looking at the trees that hid the Indian cemetery from sight. *Who were they?* I wondered. I was sad that I couldn't know but I was determined to because then they would not be as dead; their joys and sorrows would not be like the bone and dust their bodies had become.

Death was one of my most important teachers and a contributor to my lack of a childhood. Until I was nine we lived in the parsonage next door to the church, Mason Memorial Methodist. On days when Daddy would be conducting a funeral, I sat outside and waited for the hearse, which came an hour or so before the funeral began. After the undertaker and his assistants carried the coffin and flowers inside the church and came back out, I went in.

The open casket sat at the front directly below the pulpit, guarded on both sides by standing floral wreaths. I could see the profile of the deceased, who was always a church member and someone I had known. Fearfully I would walk slowly down the center aisle and stare at the person in the casket. While there was a resemblance between what I saw and the person I knew, something was missing. I wanted to find what it was and put it back so the person would be like him- or herself again. So, I would stare at the body with all the intensity an eight-year-old boy could muster and try as hard as I could to put back whatever had made the person alive. But I couldn't.

I went to funerals and the most dramatic moment for me was when the undertaker closed the casket and Daddy came down from the pulpit. The pallbearers picked up the casket by its handles and Daddy walked slowly up the center aisle, the pallbearers following, and in a loud voice, intoned, quoting scripture, "I am the resurrection and the life. He that believeth in me, though dead, yet shall he live." Even now, goose bumps rise on my arms as I can hear my father's voice and see him walking up the aisle, the pallbearers following him outside to the waiting hearse. Even though I knew that the "I" of my father's words meant Jesus, the power with which my father said the words made it seem to me as if he were the "I" who, through voice and the word alone, could bestow eternal life.

However, eternal life for me was contrasted with the brevity of temporal existence, which could be terminated in less time than it took to write this sentence, something I knew well because my childhood was littered with deaths—the friend who leaned against the passenger side door of his father's car and the door, not having been securely closed, opened and he fell out and was killed; the friend I walked to school with each day whose bathrobe caught fire as she passed the stove one winter morning, and as I walked past her house on my way to school, I knew she had burned to death little more than an hour before; the son of a family friend found sitting on a curb, a knife in his abdomen, who died without saying who stabbed him; and there was the wife of a minister, friends of our family, who was allergic to strawberries but one Sunday evening could not resist biting into their plump redness and died. The impermanence of existence was emphasized when I would overhear one of my parents say to the other, "Brother So-and-so died. He came in the house from work, had a cold drink of water, and just fell dead." Death was a neighbor and, before you realized, he could sneak through your back door and be sitting at the dinner table, knife and fork in his hands, a paper napkin tucked in his shirt.

I felt close to the dead, perhaps because they had no one to care for them, no one to listen to the stories they still needed to tell about who they were and where they had been and what they had seen. Even as a child I liked cemeteries. When I was nine we moved from the parsonage to a house a half block from a cemetery. I liked going there and walking among the tombstones, always careful never to step on a grave if I could help it. I would read the names to myself as if that mere act constituted a momentary resurrection, and I imagined those lying beneath smiling with gratitude that at least their names continued in time and there was one person who wanted to know what it had been like to be them.

I still spend a lot of time wondering about the dead and that past which was their present. As a child

I tried to imagine what was it like for de Soto when he first saw the Mississippi River; what did those natives on a small island in the Caribbean see when the masts of the *Niña, Pinta,* and *Santa Maria* came into view over the curved back of the ocean? And what was it like for those unknown and now nameless African ancestors of mine when they were pushed down the plank off a ship and they stood for the first time on the soil of this land?

"What was it like to . . . ?" Regardless of how one ends that question, the answer is always a story. Sometimes that story is classified as literature; other times it is classified as history. But in their essence, literature and history are merely stories seeking to help us understand who we are, where we have been, and where we might go.

Writing from and about the past is my way of telling stories about the present because the past is not something completed and forever pinioned to memory. The past is the accretion of known and unknown lives from whom I came and to whom I am indebted and for whom I am responsible. Nothing I feel has not been felt by many people in many times and places. Loves and hatreds do not change their natures, their ways of entwining in and around people's lives. Those Kaw Indians in the cemetery next to the library knew joy and sorrow. The sight of a herd of buffalo gave them more joy than it would me, but the warmth and elation of joy belongs to us both. It is through story that I share my knowledge of past as present, of past as presence, of past as evermore.

My father, Rev. W. D. Lester, Sr.

No one in the world knew what truth was till some-
body had told a story.

Rudyard Kipling

Story is fundamental to our psychological and spiritual lives. Descartes wanted us to believe we are
defined by our minds—"I think; therefore I am." But
even before we think, we engage in story. Story has
a unique power to involve us. The almost hypnotic
appeal of mass entertainment—television, music
videos, film—is that it tells us stories in which we
see ourselves, sometimes as we are, sometimes as
we would like to be, sometimes as we hope we will
never be.

Story is who we are. We start each day deciding
what to wear, and when we do we know what role
we want/need to play that day. When people dress
to go on a date, they dress according to the story-
line in which they want to involve each other—or
not. Perhaps marriages start to decline when
spouses stop dressing in ways that invite each other

into a story, or when their stories have become boring and they don't care enough to try and write new ones.

We are not only participants in the stories we create about ourselves, we are also participants in the stories others tell about us, stories they are convinced are true though they do not know us. If the stories are told often enough and by enough people, they become part of our identity.

In 1959 I was a student at San Diego State College in California for a semester and one of my classes was quite boring. It met at 9:00 A.M. and I was generally asleep five minutes later. One day the professor (white) woke me up. I opened my eyes to see him looking at me sympathetically as he asked, "Do you come from a large family?"

I knew immediately what story the professor was in and what my lines were, so I said, "Yes, sir." (I never had a problem saying "yes, sir" or "yes, ma'am" to whites if they were going to do me a favor.)

"And are you putting yourself through school?"

"Yes, sir."

"You work nights?"

"Yes, sir."

"Well, I understand. If you have to sleep in my class, it's all right."

I thanked him and went back to sleep and got an A for the course. (If I'd been a white student in that class I would have hated me.) Instead of respecting me enough to ask for my story, he saw my skin color and thought he knew all there was to know.

Each of us creates stories about ourselves and others; each of us participates in stories created by others, often people we have never met. Political leaders make decisions that affect the lives of millions of people on the basis of information. But how that information is understood and interpreted is based on story. A story about Jews evolved through centuries of European history and culminated in the murders of six million men, women, and children. A story was created around the black skin of Africans and untold millions died or were enslaved.

Story can express profound truths as well as untruths. A child will say, "Tell me a story," and yet when the child does something he shouldn't have, we say, "What happened? And don't you dare tell me a story!"

At its best, story provides us with ways to see ourselves, ways to affirm our struggles to overcome adversities, ways to help us reach out to others and forge relationships. When a child says, "Tell me a story," the child understands that story is far more than words. The telling of a story is an event in which the child may sit on the storyteller's lap and as her body relaxes into that of the teller, the child knows she will have the full attention of the teller. Story creates an intimacy that is remembered in mind, body, and soul for a lifetime. We may forget most of the stories that are told or read to us when we are children, but we remember who told it, what his or her voice sounded like, the smells and sounds in the house, classroom, or library. In the story-telling experience we bind ourselves to others. In so doing we overcome a measure of that loneliness inherent in the human condition. We need to share our stories because in so doing we hope to be understood and being understood we are no longer so alone.

I was fascinated by the title of a book that came out in 1999—*Monica's Story.* How poignant. Monica's story. For over a year everybody in America talked about Monica Lewinsky. We all had our versions of her story and very strong opinions about who she was and her sexual relationship with the President of the United States of America. Yet, scarcely any of us had heard even the sound of her voice. When she finally spoke, what else could she call her book except *Monica's Story*? By telling her story, she hoped to evoke feelings of recognition and empathy and, in so doing, relieve what must have been and may continue to be an extraordinary loneliness. Through story we seek to know ourselves and we seek to be known. Thus we become joined with others.

Grave of Samuel Altschul,
my great-great-grandfather

Grave of Adolph Altschul,
my great-grandfather

Grave of Maggie Altschul, my great-grandmother

The universe is made of stories—not atoms.

Muriel Ruykeyser

Story is the fundamental language of our lives. Every evening in practically every home in America the same question is asked: "How was your day?" It is more than a query into how someone is feeling. We are asking (and being asked) for a story about what we did, who we saw, what they talked about, and what we said in response.

Anytime we open our mouths and say, "Did you hear what happened to So-and-so?" we are about to tell a story. We have been educated to believe stories begin with "Once upon a time." I am convinced the first stories began differently.

Imagine a child running in the house and yelling, "Mom! Guess what happened to Little Red Riding Hood?" Imagine what the neighbors said 3,000 years ago about two brothers: "Girl, you won't believe this, but you know old man Isaac? He's got them two boys,

Jacob and Esau. Well, he's been sick, you know, and lost his sight a year or so ago, poor thing, and he thought he was about to die and wanted to give his blessing to the oldest boy, Esau, which is the way it's supposed to be. Well, Isaac's wife, Rebecca, heard about it. She wanted the younger boy, Jacob, to have the blessing and she fixed it so that's what happened! Can you imagine a mother tricking her husband and her oldest boy so the youngest one could get the blessing? Well, I never did like that hussy anyway."

I love listening to people tell stories about their lives. A few years before my father died in the summer of 1981 he said to me, "You should write a book about my life." Like many children who take their parents for granted, I didn't see a story in my father's life. The day of his funeral after we returned from the mausoleum where he was interred, my mother asked if I would clean out his study, which had been my room through high school and college.

As I began emptying my father's desk I found a folder in the middle drawer. Inside were drafts my father had written for his obituary. There were five and with each one the handwriting became progressively shakier. Suddenly, it was as if I had left my body because I was looking down from the ceiling on an old black man sitting at his desk, pen in hand, trying to find the words to summarize his life. That was the moment I began thinking about writing a novel based on my father's life.

However, almost catatonic with grief, I was unable to write. Early that fall I was in my office at the university getting ready to go teach a class when I noticed something strange. I could not blink my left eye. When I got to class I realized only the right side of my mouth moved. The left side of my face was paralyzed!

When I went to the doctor he said I had Bell's Palsy, facial paralysis, and the condition would correct itself over time. The most illuminating piece of information, however, came from Rebecca Dobkins, a student in one of my classes. She showed me a passage in a book about the Apaches she'd been reading for an anthropology class. The Apaches believed that paralysis of the facial muscles indicated that a person's body had been taken over by the spirit of a dead person. The implication for me was obvious. My father was insisting I write the book about his life.

The vision I'd had of the old black man sitting at his desk trying to write his obituary became the opening paragraph of my novel *Do Lord Remember Me* (Holt, 1984; St. Martin's Press, 2004). In imagining my father's story I came to see that the span of his life from his birth on November 5, 1897, to his death on July 31, 1981, actually covered a broader spectrum of time. His memory, at least as I imagined it, included the stories he might have heard from those who had been slaves. Thus, his life covered black history from slavery through the civil rights movement. (My facial paralysis eased as I began the novel and gradually went away as I continued to work on it. But if one looks closely at the left side of my face, there is a deep crease going from my nostril and down past my mouth. I call it the mark of my father.) In writing *Do Lord Remember Me* I learned that our lives incorporate more than our physical existence and personal memories. Generations abide within us, something I had unknowingly learned as a child.

I was around eight or nine and was walking with my parents along a street in downtown Pine Bluff, Arkansas, one hot summer day when, on a store window I saw the name Altschul. That was the name on my grandmother's mailbox, Altschul being her maiden name and the surname of her brother, Rudolph, with whom she lived.

"That's the name on Grandmama's mailbox," I said excitedly.

"Those are your cousins," my father told me.

I didn't understand. The store was owned by white people. How could they be my cousins? Daddy told me a story about a man named Adolph Altschul who immigrated from Germany to Pine Bluff with his father, brothers, and a sister, sometime before the

Civil War. After the war Adolph met an ex-slave, a tall, fair-skinned woman named Maggie Carson. She and Adolph fell in love but in that time and place they could not marry legally. But they lived together as husband and wife and eventually had six children, one of whom was my grandmother Emma Altschul Smith, another of whom was her brother, my great-uncle Rudolph. My father concluded the story with words that changed my life: "Your great-grandfather was a Jew."

At the moment of hearing those words I cannot say I knew that I would one day convert to Judaism, a spiritual odyssey I related in *Lovesong: Becoming a Jew* (Arcade, 1988). But I realized immediately that I would be a different person if someone else had been my great-grandfather.

Sadly, sometimes all that remains of a story is a name—Adolph Altschul. His letters and photographs of him and my great-grandmother were lost when my grandmother's house burned. So, I do not know how tall he was and what he looked like or even what he did for a living. (As I recount in *Lovesong*, I did learn he played trumpet in the Confederate Army band, which I find very amusing.) However, my mother remembered that when her father died, Adolph came and got her, her mother, and her siblings and brought them to live with Maggie and him for a while.

I know only two stories about my great-grandmother Maggie. My cousin Dorothy remembered her as having very white, almost porcelainlike skin, and she always wore a black apron and served tea and cookies every day at four o'clock. I don't think there's any question she had been a house slave and loved social ritual.

The other story was from my mother. When Adolph was dying, he asked Maggie to get word to his brothers and sister. They had disowned him for "marrying"... what? An ex-slave, or a Gentile? I wish I knew. But when he died, Maggie somehow got word to them and they came with the rabbi and took his body and buried him in the Jewish cemetery.

I didn't understand why she would let those who had disowned him take his body. Perhaps it was important to him that he be buried among Jews. According to my mother he maintained his identity as a Jew and went to synagogue on Saturdays. I thought he should be buried next to Maggie and I wanted to dig up his body and bury him where I thought he belonged. Yet, she had chosen otherwise. Why?

One of the extraordinary dimensions of story is what we perceive to be only a personal story is sometimes linked to stories almost as ancient as human existence. One motivating factor in my conversion to Judaism was that I felt compelled to reach back through space and time and grasp my great-grandfather's hand and bring him back into the family whose progenitor he'd been. Many years passed before I understood that there was yet another dimension to the story.

In Exodus 13:19 there are these words: "And Moses took the bones of Joseph with him because [Joseph] had made the children of Israel swear, saying, 'God will be sure to remember you; and you shall carry up my bones from here with you.'" (Author's translation.)

The verse refers back to Genesis 50:25, when Joseph, on his death bed, extracts the promise that his bones will be taken out of Egypt when the Israelites leave for the land God was giving them. The Torah does not tell us, however, who assumed responsibility to remember the promise made to Joseph. For more than 200 years the children of Israel were enslaved and for more than 200 years someone remembered Joseph's bones. I am awed by a remembering that spanned two centuries. Jewish tradition says the person who remembered lived for more than 200 years. I prefer to believe that people in ancient times lived three-score-and-ten years, more or less, and that it was the task of a number of people to keep the promise to Joseph, a man they had never known. But, they kept his story alive, not merely as words but through their relationship to his bones.

I was the one in my family who kept the story of

Adolph Altschul alive, even though I knew scarcely more than his name. Why me? Why not my brother or any one of my many cousins, all of whom were also great-grandchildren of that German Jew? But had I not been remembering bones since childhood? Had I not taken it as my holy task not only to remember the past but, as a writer, to give it breath just as I had tried to return breath to those bodies in the coffins at my father's church, though I had not known as a child that was what I was trying to do?

March 1990. I had a speaking engagement at a synagogue in Little Rock and went a few days early so I could visit the family cemetery and see if I could find Adolph's grave in the Jewish cemetery. I had not been to Arkansas since 1982, the year after my father's death, when I took my mother to Pine Bluff for her last visit to the family cemetery, and brought my oldest son, Malcolm, for what would most likely be his only visit. I did not know the verse about Joseph's bones then but I had begun to wonder which of my children would remember our dead. My grandmother began the task. My mother told me she would light a candle on a certain day each spring. My mother didn't remember what month or why, but now I knew. It was a *yahrzeit* candle Emma lit, the candle Jews light on the anniversary of a person's death. I would later learn that her father, Adolph, died in June. My grandmother not only remembered but it was on her property that the actual bones of Adolph's wife, her mother, and four of their children were buried. After Grandmother died, my mother was the only one of her siblings who came to Pine Bluff regularly to pull grass from the earth where the bones resided. I lived too far away to visit frequently, but I remembered where the bones were. Who would remember after me?

When I got to Pine Bluff, the places I had known as a child existed only in my memory now. Where my grandmother's house had been was a huge and unsightly field of thick weeds and oppressive woods. To the east, beside the railroad tracks, had been the house of my grandmother's sister, Rena, and her husband, Fate. On the other side of the railroad tracks had been a lumber mill whose whistle had marked noon and five o'clock.

The mill was gone, as was Aunt Rena's house. The gravel roads had been replaced by paved streets. I found the dead-end street at the back of Grandmother's property and parked when I could drive no farther. I got out of the car and followed a barely visible path into the woods.

Arkansas had been inundated with rain that spring and the earth was soggy. Even though it had been eight years since I'd been there, I remembered that the way to find the family cemetery was to look for trash.

Almost as a bulwark against the dead, the neighbors had dumped beer cans, old furniture, bed springs, and unidentifiable detritus near the family cemetery. When I saw rusting beer cans I knew I was close.

The family cemetery was in a clearing behind a sagging wire fence. Mother had granite tombstones put on each grave but some of them had sunk so far into the soft earth that only the name and date of birth were visible. Behind each tombstone was a pot of yellow plastic flowers Mother placed there who knew how many years past.

I stood for a while at each grave, wishing they would tell me all they knew about their father and mother, my grand-grandfather, the German Jew, and my great-grandmother, the freed slave, the daughter of a Virginia plantation owner and a slave woman.

RUDOLPH ALTSCHUL
JANUARY 24, 1883

Uncle Rudolph was tall with stooped rounded shoulders. He never married and lived with his sister, my grandmother. I never knew what he did for a living. During my childhood he was already retired and spent his days in his rocking chair, starting on the porch in the morning and following the shade around the house until he was back on the porch when evening came. Each Saturday he went to town and once he brought me back a sack of oranges. He was the most silent person I have ever known. All the words I ever heard him speak would not make a half-page of double-spaced text. Near the end of his life he had an argument with Grandmother and moved out of the house into a shed a few yards away. However, he came into the house each day at noon to eat, as his sister continued cooking for him, but he died without ever speaking to her again.

CHARLIE ALTSCHUL
1879–1965

He was also tall, but unlike Uncle Rudolph, there was a dignity in the way Uncle Charlie carried himself. He lived in Chicago and I had vague memories of a small, stifling-hot apartment and a man who looked like a white man and being told he was my "uncle Charlie." He, too, was quiet. He lived with a large, black-skinned woman whom we called "Miss Sophie." If he had married her I would have called her "Aunt Sophie." All I remember about her is that she liked to fish.

IRENE MCGOWAN
[DATES BELOW THE SURFACE]
FAYETTE MCGOWAN
[DATES BELOW THE SURFACE]

Aunt Rena and her husband, Uncle Fate. They had been against Mother marrying my father because

"That nigger is too black," they said. In their final years, however, it was my father who supported them. Aunt Rena was deaf when I knew her and her primary activity was cursing her husband, who was blind. I understood what hell was the day Uncle Fate said to me, "Son, you know she's deaf and she cusses me all day and night and I can't cuss her back 'cause she can't hear." I spent a lot of time with him one summer so he would have someone who could hear his voice and he could hear a voice that was not filled with malice. I sat by his bed and read magazines to him, *Police Gazette* and the like. Only now, as I write, do I remember that was how my predilection for reading about murders began.

EMMA L. SMITH

JULY 19, 1873

FEB. 9, 1965

Grandmother. She was a thin woman with enormous hands who talked to herself continually, much of the time in profanity.

It is a sacred task to remember. One does not have to remember specifics. My memories of Uncle Rudolph, Uncle Charlie, Aunt Rena, Uncle Fate, and Grandmother are few, but remembering even their names is to tend their souls.

Adolph's wife, my great-grandmother.

There were other tombstones of Adolph and Maggie's children here—an Aunt Ada, whom I never knew or heard any stories about, and an old and worn tombstone that seemed to be the grave of a child. But the decades of weather had worn away the stone until the lettering was illegible.

One of Adolph and Maggie's children was not buried here. That was Aunt Florence. She moved to Indiana and except for a postcard and one visit in the middle of the night, no one ever heard from her, an indication, everyone agreed, that she had decided to pass for white. No one in the family condemned her for doing so.

I walked around the property looking for any trace of the house, the chicken yard, or the outhouse. Where there had been family and memories and sorrows and fears and courage, there were now only weeds and trees and underbrush. Time could alter space, render it unrecognizable, make it appear as if you never were. I went back to the car and drove away along streets where there had been only woods forty years before.

I wanted to find the Jewish cemetery. I stopped at a filling station and asked directions. All I got was a look of confusion when I said I was looking for the "Jewish cemetery." It took me a moment before I remembered that I was in the South. I slowed my speech, found my southern accent and the rules of southern grammar, and said, "I'm looking for where the Jews are buried at." Comprehension was instantaneous and the directions were immediately forthcoming.

I came to a large cemetery with crosses adorning the tombstones. I drove through slowly, baffled. This was obviously not the Jewish cemetery, *nor* where the Jews were buried. There was a monument business across the street and I drove over and asked the man inside.

"The Jews are buried in the back of that cemetery."

I returned and at the very rear, separated from the Christians by a roadway, was the Jewish cemetery.

Water stood almost shoe-top high in places, while elsewhere the ground was so soggy it squished beneath my feet. The older section of the Jewish cemetery was recognizable by the weathered tombstones that did not glisten in the sunlight, but they possessed a presence and substance the modern ones did not.

I stopped before a tall, imposing old tombstone. The grave itself covered by a stone slab. I was startled when I read the name:

SAML ALTSCHUL

BORN AT OBERLUSTADT. RHEINPFALZ

DIED AT PINE BLUFF. ARK.

DEC. 7. 1878;

AGED 62 YRS.

Here were the bones of my great-great-grandfather, Adolph's father.

At the top of the tombstone, within a circle, were
carved two hands, thumbs touching, and the first two
and last two fingers on each hand were separated. This
was the sign of the kohanim, which Leonard Nimoy as
Mr. Spock had made popular on the original *Star Trek*
television series, though Nimoy had used only one
hand. Kohanim had been the priests at the Temple in
Jerusalem and were descendants of Aaron, the brother
of Moses. Today, a kohain is the first person called to
the Torah in Orthodox and Conservative synagogues.
Kohanim also bless the congregation by making the
sign and reciting the Kohanic Blessing—"May the Lord
bless you and keep you; May the Lord make His face
shine upon you and be gracious to you; May the Lord
lift up His face upon you and give you peace."

Kohanic lineage is passed from father to son. I was
not a kohain but there was no mistaking that my life
was encircled by men who occupied places of ritual
symbolism—my minister father and his minister father

and Samuel and Adolph, the descendants of Aaron. Was it any wonder that my life was so God-obsessed?

Beneath the sign of the kohanim were some lines of Hebrew. I could not translate them all but they seemed to be describing him as a "righteous and upright man" whose name was "Shmuel ben Yissachar HaKohein"—Samuel the son of Yissachar the Kohein. So, Yissachar was the Hebrew name of my great-great-great-grandfather. The Hebrew inscription gave the date of Samuel's death as the eleventh of Kislev. The Hebrew year was there but I didn't know Hebrew numbers well enough. I wondered if my great-grandfather had come to the burial of his father and, eleven months later, the unveiling of this massive tombstone.

I continued through the old part of the Jewish cemetery looking for Adolph's grave. I was getting frustrated and annoyed at being unable to find his grave. I came to a pool of water separating two rows of tombstones. As I was trying to decide if I could leap over the water, a pair of hands grabbed my shoulders (though no one was there) and spun me around. The "hands" pushed my head down. There, at my feet was the tombstone of my great-grandfather.

ADOLPH ALTSCHUL

BORN IN

OBERLUSTADT

RHEINPFALZ.

DIED IN
PINE BLUFF. ARK.
JUNE 11. 1901.
AGED 60 YEARS.

I burst into tears and I heard myself addressing him, saying, inexplicably, "I came back. I came back." Inside myself I felt as if a large circle that had been trying to complete itself for almost a century had now done so. I didn't know what that was, but it was more than the "return" to Judaism my conversion represented. It had something to do with him—Adolph Altschul and who he had been—and me.

If there was any member of the family who was my spiritual ancestor, it was Adolph. He had defied convention, the law, his religion, and his family to live with the woman he loved. He had known that more important than what others thought of you, more important than what the law could do to you, more important than your family's love, and more important than what your religion said was moral and immoral was taking the risk to live your inner truth, regardless of the consequences. God wanted that even more than obedience to the codes of collective morality He decreed. Inner truth was its own authority and only you and God might understand. Sometimes, only God did. At least I hoped He did because, most of the time, I knew I didn't.

My great-grandfather's tombstone was as unimposing as his father's was grandiose. It was a small slab of stone cut at a forty-five-degree angle and resting atop a piled circle of thin stones. So much love and respect was lavished on the tombstone of the father. There was no love on that of Adolph. Most disappointing was the absence of a Hebrew inscription that would have given me his Hebrew name.

I started crying again as I placed a stone on Adolph's headstone. "I came back," I said again. "I came back." I did not understand why I was saying that I had come back to a place I had never been. I placed a stone also on my great-great-grandfather's gravestone and left.

I drove back to the family cemetery. I needed to stand before those graves again. Now more than ever I wished they could tell me all I wanted to know about our family's story, but they were silent. I didn't know why, but I found myself standing in front of Maggie's grave. I wanted to leave but, for some reason, was unable to. I had lived with myself long enough to trust that I should remain standing there. I waited. Suddenly, I knew! Had Maggie told me?

I ran to the car and noted the mileage on the odometer. I drove hurriedly to the Jewish cemetery. The odometer indicated that I had gone only three miles. I went to my great-grandfather's grave and looked in the direction of my great-grandmother's grave. In my mind, the buildings and stores and neon signs and highway were no longer there and I saw the landscape as if it had been forty years ago, as it was eighty years ago when one could have walked in a straight line from the house where my grandmother and great-grandmother lived to this grave. The distance was not more than a mile or so. I started laughing and crying simultaneously. That was why she let them take his body to be buried in the Jewish cemetery. He would be only a short walk away in the cool of the evening.

Joseph said God would remember them if they remembered his bones.

The act of remembering establishes a relationship to truth, for there is no truth if we do not know that we are the bridge from the known and unknown past to the uncreated future. If we do not remember well the past—known and unknown—the future will be born in anger.

I returned to the Jewish cemetery and placed another stone on my great-grandfather's grave. I could not take his bones with me but I took stones from that circle on which his tombstone rested, put them in my pocket and walked slowly away.

Tomkins Square Park, New York City, 1966

*Why does anybody tell a story? It does indeed have
something to do with faith, faith that the universe
has meaning, that our little human lives are not
irrelevant, that what we choose or say or do matters,
matters cosmically.*

Madeleine L'Engle, Walking on Water

Each of us is comprised of stories, stories not only
about ourselves but stories about ancestors we never
knew and people we've never met. We have stories we
love to tell and stories we have never told anyone. The
extent to which others know us is determined by the
stories we choose to share. We extend a deep trust to
someone when we say, "I'm going to tell you something I've never told anyone." Sharing stories creates
trust because through stories we come to a recognition
of how much we have in common.

I have a fantasy that peace will come to the Middle
East only when small groups of Jews and Arabs sit in
circles and tell each other stories about who they are
and what they do and who their parents and grandparents were. No one would be permitted to talk about
what he *believed*. No one would be permitted to offer
an *opinion* about anything or anyone. You could only

tell stories about yourself and those whose bones you are guarding. You could only listen to stories about others and the bones in their care.

In my first significant relationships with whites I was fortunate that neither they nor I knew anything about racial politics. Negroes had not yet become black or African-American, the words creating a different story line than that represented by "colored" and Negro. The latter bespoke a story line inclusive of whites and considered it reason for celebration when a white person expressed an interest in knowing us as fellow human beings.

My alma mater, Fisk University in Nashville, had an exchange program with a number of small, white liberal-arts colleges—Oberlin, Pomona, Wooster, Beloit, and Colby, among others—who sent two students to Fisk for a semester while two Fisk students went to their schools. When I think back to my college years from 1956 to 1960, I love who we were. We did not think then of ourselves as participants in rewriting a story that had been told for centuries about who blacks and whites were, but that is what we did.

There was no one telling us how we were supposed to be with each other and what we were supposed to say or not say. So, we did what came naturally; we told each other stories about our young lives. In doing so we gave of ourselves.

I lived at home throughout my four years in college and my parents became nervous when I told them I had white friends. They were frightened for me, for my safety, but they accepted that I wanted to write a story different from the familiar one they knew in which blacks and whites were antagonists. So, when I would bring an exchange student home for Sunday dinner, they acted as if having a white person in their home was something they had been doing for years.

Some exchange students had difficulty being in the minority for the first time in their lives. The key to a white exchange student's acceptance by us was whether that student lived our story as blacks in Nashville, Tennessee. That meant not taking advantage of their whiteness by riding at the front of a bus, or going downtown to eat at a restaurant or see a movie, or doing anything that came naturally to them because they were white and had never had to think about where they could and could not go, what they could and could not do.

I admired those exchange students—Candie Anderson, Leslie Green, Pat Downes, Nancy Rowe, Joanie Blank, Barbara Johnson, Jim Zwerg, Cynthia Perrine, and the others whose names I've forgotten. They made our stories their own. They had not only exchanged schools, they exchanged lives, identities, ways of being. That is the challenge inherent in listening to another's story. How willing am I to exchange my story for someone else's?

I taught for thirty-two years and each semester when I walked into a classroom for the first time I was overwhelmed by the fact that each student represented a story. How could I be a good teacher if I did not know their stories? Their stories determined what they heard and how they heard it. During that first class I would ask them to write an autobiography telling me where they were from, what they were studying, why they were in the class, and, finally, anything they would like me to know about themselves. Some of the stories they told belied their appearances as happy, untroubled, and carefree youths. One wrote of being ten years old and coming home from school and finding her mother dead of a heart attack as she had started to dress for work; another young woman's boyfriend had been killed in a car accident a month before school opened; one young man was very angry because he was going blind at age nineteen; and so many students wrote about alcoholic and sexually abusive parents.

It helped me to know something of everyone's story because often personal questions were asked in a disinterested and academic way. But if I knew something of the student's story, then perhaps I could hear that something deeply personal was being asked in a seemingly harmless question. "What do you mean?" was merely curiosity when asked by one student. From another, it was desperation.

It was equally important that I told students stories about my life. Students heard about my children, former girlfriends, ex-wives, and who knows what else. Many academics consider it improper to tell students about their personal lives. But when I think about my education I don't consciously remember the knowledge my teachers imparted, but I have vivid memories of them as people. A teacher is not merely an intellect dispensing knowledge. I consist of stories whose power in my life is far more compelling than mere intellect could ever be. My personal story influenced how I taught as well as what I emphasized as important for students to know.

When I read my students' stories and when they listened to mine over the course of a semester, we created an I-Thou relationship in which a part of who they were is now part of me and some of who I am is now part of them. Story makes us more human to each other.

Cotton Field, Mississippi, 1966

[The art of the novel] happens because the story-teller's own experience of men and things, whether for good or ill—not only what he has passed through himself, but even events which he has only witnessed or been told of—has moved him to an emotion so passionate that he can no longer keep it shut up in his heart.

Murasaki Shikibu, *The Tale of the Genji*

When I am asked what advice I would give someone who wants to write, my first response is: Read, read, read. When I read students' attempts at creative writing it is obvious immediately that most of them have not read much or widely. The aspiring writer must read everything he or she can to appreciate the myriad ways words are used and to what effect. Virginia Woolf, James Joyce, and William Faulkner each used stream of consciousness, but in different ways. What are those differences? How did each writer's way of using stream of consciousness serve what she or he wrote? How is a popular writer like Stephen King able to make you believe what you know rationally cannot exist, and yet anyone reading his novel *Christine* never again looks at a car in the same way.

Besides reading I have learned a lot about writing from music and art. I played piano from age five through college and performed a two-piano arrangement of the first movement of the Bach Concerto in D Minor at a school convocation with my girlfriend Janeice Cochran. I also studied voice, sang bass in the college choir, which sang a chorale I wrote, and gave a voice recital on which I sang folk songs and played guitar. (I had a brief career as a folk singer in the 1960s and recorded two albums of spirituals and original songs for Vanguard Records.)

The study and appreciation of music has heightened my sensitivity to sound and voice so much that sometimes I conceive of a book as a set of variations on a theme as Brahms and Rachmaninoff did with a theme of Paganini's. I usually listen to music while I write, and what I listen to will influence the writing. Johann Sebastian Bach's music makes me try to write sentences as clean and articulated as the lines of a fugue, while the melodies of Chopin and Tchaikovsky make me want to write lines so achingly beautiful that the reader will burst into tears. My wife claims that the sound of my typing often mirrors the flow of the music itself. I haven't figured out what the relationship is between writing and my love of movie scores but at various times I have written to the music from *The Godfather, Love Story, Schindler's List,* and, most recently, *Crouching Tiger, Hidden Dragon.* (This book is being written to a mélange of Bach, Handel, Chopin, Tchaikovsky, and Eva Cassidy.)

I began studying art in high school, primarily because my homeroom teacher, Nathan Holiday, who was also the art teacher, would not accept that anyone could not draw and paint. Although I was not very talented, he helped me develop what little ability I had. I minored in art at Fisk, primarily so I could study with Aaron Douglas, who had been the leading artist of the Harlem Renaissance of the 1920s. That spring semester of my senior year I had a small exhibit of paintings and drawings. Although I have drawn and painted intermittently in the years since, my need to be creative visually found expression in photography, a passion since childhood that involves me more deeply now than ever.

Studying art taught me how to rewrite. When drawing with charcoal, a black tone is not created all at once. You begin with light grays, and by applying more and more layers of gray a black tone is eventually achieved in gradations of tone. The same is true in watercolor painting where colors are layered until there is a flow from the lightest saturations of color to the most vibrant. So, when I rewrite I visualize myself back in the art studio at Fisk, hunched over a drawing board, delicately shading a charcoal drawing.

The study and appreciation of art has also helped

me learn to see. My wife and I go to museums and galleries as often as we can to educate our eyes and souls to what is possible when you allow your spirit to swim deep into the realm of the imagination.

During my college years I considered making a career of music or art but neither came as easily to me as writing. I had an instinct for words, which are so real to me that I feel like I hold them in my hands and assess their weight and shape before deciding which ones to put on the page. Other times words are like colored grains of sand and I am not so much writing as creating a mosaic or sand painting. I also have a patience with words that I lacked with music and art. My piano playing could be sloppy because I didn't want to devote the necessary time to reworking a phrase until I had found the best fingering. When I drew I knew what I was supposed to do to create a rich charcoal black but I could be impatient making layer after layer of gray. After I began photographing seriously I loved spending eight to ten hours in the darkroom making prints but I did not have the patience of a W. Eugene Smith, who took eight hours to make *one* print (but now I am learning). However, I will rewrite a sentence, paragraph, page, twenty-five, thirty, and more times.

Looking back I am simultaneously awed and embarrassed by my bravado and arrogance in deciding to become a writer. Nothing I wrote during my college years supported such a decision. My parents certainly thought I had taken leave of my senses when I told them what I wanted to do with my life. My father still had a faint hope that I would follow him and his father into the ministry and I considered applying to the University of Chicago's School of Religion for its program in religion and literature, but I was tired of having to read what someone else wanted me to read. My mother had no career ambitions for me other than that I get a job, any job. Both of my parents tried to convince me that I could have a job and write at nights and on the weekends.

I was afraid that pursuing a career would entrap me in the values of a society where commerce was more important than the unfolding of the soul, so I made it a point to quit a job whenever I was offered a promotion and/or a raise. I was afraid of being seduced by the ego-gratification of a title and money. I was more afraid, however, of looking at my life in twenty years and wondering why I had not had the courage to try and live my dream.

A year after I moved to New York City in 1961, earning money became less problematic when I married Joan Steinau, a young woman who was happy to work if I took care of the house and cooked, which I did gladly. I supplemented our income by teaching folk guitar and banjo, and I wrote.

For four years after graduation I wrote haiku, short stories, novellas, and sent manuscripts to literary publications such as *Paris Review.* Among the form rejection letters I received with discouraging regularity was a personal note from Rose Styron, fiction editor of *Paris Review* at the time, who wanted to see other stories I might write. This word of encouragement from someone who didn't know me helped on the days when I became almost convinced that I was deluding myself in thinking I could write.

The problem facing most young writers is, what to write about? Writers are told to write what they know. That may seem obvious but it isn't. Being young, I was not convinced I knew anything. Or perhaps it was that I had no interest in writing about what I knew—race. Richard Wright, Ralph Ellison, and James Baldwin had covered that territory very well. What on earth could I add? Besides haiku, I don't recall what I wrote during those four years but I knew I was floundering. While I was certainly gaining valuable experience in putting words to paper and learning much about the craft of writing, the finished pieces did not live. I felt like that eight-year-old boy standing before the open caskets in his father's church trying to give soul to the dead.

84

I would not become a writer until I found my sub-ject. A writer can certainly have more than one subject over a lifetime, but that initial one opens the gate and grants admission to that element of soul uniquely his or hers to give expression to.

Often artists find their initial subject matter in the place(s) where they have been most deeply wounded. Paradoxically, it is here our soul's energy coalesces into a throbbing which can be treated only by creative transmutation. My subject had been living with me since childhood and I had not recognized it.

I was around seven or eight when a colorful brochure came in the mail from a company offering to research the Lester family tree and send us our family coat of arms. When I saw that my father was going to discard the brochure I asked anxiously, "Don't you want to know our family history?"

Daddy laughed dryly. "I don't need to pay any-body to tell me where we came from. Our family tree ends in a bill of sale. Lester is the name of the family that owned us."

That was as defining a moment in my life as learn-ing my maternal great-grandfather was a Jew. In both instances my child-self was confronted by the silence of the dead, a silence I refused to accept. I had an intense need to get past that bill of sale. I accepted that the Lesters would never have a coat of arms, but a bill of sale instead? No! The summer of 1964 I awoke to my subject when I went to Mississippi as part of what the civil rights movement called the Mississippi Summer Project.

Nineteen sixty-four was the year it became obvious that America was undergoing significant change. Mario Savio, a student leader of the Free Speech Movement at the University of California in Berkeley, identified the nature of that change at a rally in the fall when he said there was "a growing understanding among many people in America that history had not ended, that a better society is possible, and that it is worth dying for . . . an important minority of men and women coming to the front today have shown that they will die rather than be standardized, replaceable and irrelevant."

My own aversion to a "career" that would give me a title and money in exchange for my soul was part of a generational questioning of values that began with the Beat Generation in the late 1950s and the writings of John Clellon Holmes, Jack Kerouac, Gary Snyder, and Allen Ginsberg. I had a vivid memory of reading Allen Ginsberg's "Howl" in that now famous second issue of *Evergreen Review.* I had a deep, visceral response to lines referring to people Ginsberg described as "angel-headed hipsters"

> ...who passed through universities with radiant cool eyes hallu-
> cinating Arkansas and Blake-light tragedy among the
> scholars of war,
> who were expelled from the academies for crazy & publishing
> obscene odes on the windows of the skull

and

> Moloch whose love is endless oil and stone! Moloch whose
> soul is electricity and banks! Moloch whose poverty
> is the specter of genius! Moloch whose fate is a cloud
> of sexless hydrogen! Moloch whose name is the Mind!

I did not pretend to understand every line, at least not intellectually, but I did understand in a place where words did not matter. The Beat Generation, the civil rights movement, the anti–Vietnam War movement were about more than mere social change. We were daring to try and change the values by which American society defined itself and us, and that was something worth dying for. And people died.

Although President Lyndon Johnson signed the 1964 Civil Rights Act that summer outlawing segregation in public accommodations, it was too little, too late, and blacks rioted in many urban centers in the Northeast, including New York's Harlem, and people died. In June, at the start of the Mississippi Summer Project, three young men, who were part of that summer's efforts to register blacks in Mississippi to vote, disappeared near Philadelphia, Mississippi. Those of us who knew anything about Mississippi knew that James Chaney, Andrew Goodman, and Michael Schwerner were dead, though their bodies would not be found until August.

For most of my thirty-two-year academic career I taught courses on the 1960s and, in an attempt to communicate something of what that time was like for many of us, I sometimes asked my students to write a paper reflecting on the question "What would I die for?" I explained that I was really asking them to reflect on their values. Did they define life as physical, i.e., the beating of the heart in their chests, or was there a spiritual dimension to life, an ideal, which, if threatened, would take precedence over their heartbeats? Even though Massachusetts is a very Catholic state and many, if not most, of my students grew up in the Catholic church, very few of them grasped the central concept of Christianity, namely, that life is not worth living at *all* costs, that under some circumstances, a physical death can be a spiritual affirmation.

"Am I willing to die for this?" was the question anyone who went south to work in the civil rights movement had to answer for himself. Did any of us *want* to die? Of course not. Would we *seek* death? Of course not. Would we do everything in our power to avoid dying? Absolutely. Would we be willing to die because realizing the ideal of a society based on principles of equality and love was worth more than our lives? Well, if we didn't have any choice, okay.

About 1,000 college-age students went to Mississippi that summer to participate in voter registration campaigns, or teach in what were called "freedom schools" where black children learned about the history of their people for the first time in their lives. I went as a folk singer, one of many—Pete Seeger, Joan Baez, Bob Cohen, Judy Collins, Barbara Dane, Len Chandler, and the late Gil Turner—who traveled around the state for varying periods of time to lead singing at mass meetings, teach songs at freedom schools, and give concerts.

I was there for two weeks and even before I boarded the Greyhound bus in New York for Jackson, Mississippi, I knew my going was for more reasons than those represented by the Mississippi Summer Project. Mississippi was the state in which the bill of sale had been signed and we were given the name Lester. I was going to the home of my slave ancestors. They were waiting for me.

It was a blazing hot July day. I was standing at the edge of a field in Laurel, Mississippi. I don't recall how I happened to be standing there. I only remember that I was. Suddenly, it was not 1964 but 1854 or 1844 and I was a slave who paused from working the cotton to lean on my hoe. Gazing northward I wonder: What was on the other side of the horizon line far in the distance? If I could walk to that line and step across it, would I be free? What would that feel like? To be free? I stare for a while longer. Then, not wanting to think about it anymore and before the overseer notices me looking off into space and lays his whip across my sweaty back, I go back to hoeing.

Just as suddenly as I had been possessed, I was returned to myself wondering: *Who was that man staring at the horizon? What had it been like to be him? What had it been like to be a slave?*

I am convinced that the spot on which I stood that July day was the same spot on which a slave had stood more than a hundred years before and his spirit had entered me. Though I did not know his name, I knew I had to tell his story and as many stories as I could of those who had been slaves. I had uncovered my subject. I had been chosen to carry Joseph's bones.

That autumn I began researching slave narratives. I went to the Library of Congress in Washington, D.C., and read through many of the Federal Writers Project interviews made with former slaves in the 1930s. In them I found descriptions of every aspect of plantation life as well as vivid stories that conveyed what it had been like to be a slave. I was hoping to find interviews with my slave ancestors. I didn't, but my disappointment was mitigated by realizing that my wound was not unique. Intrinsic to the genealogy of most American blacks was a bill of sale. I wanted to write a book in which those who had been slaves spoke for themselves. In so doing I thought I would take away the shame which gnawed at the innards of their descendants and put that shame on white America where it rightfully belonged.

In the course of my research I learned of narratives written in the nineteenth century by escaped slaves which abolitionists used in the fight to end slavery. University Place Bookshop in Manhattan specialized in black history and literature and I bought original editions of slave narratives for very little money, as well as a volume that had belonged to W. E. B. DuBois. My research yielded enough material for a book on what slavery had been like in the words of those who had been slaves. However, the one publisher I approached showed no interest. Afraid that another rejection would cause me to lose faith in the idea, I continued doing research but made no further attempt to secure a publisher.

In the fall of 1966 I published an essay in *Sing Out!* magazine called "The Angry Children of Malcolm X." In it I described the new and angry mood among blacks, something I knew well because I had begun working full time that year for the Student Nonviolent

Coordinating Committee (SNCC) as head of its photography department in Atlanta, Georgia. SNCC was the most outspoken of the civil rights groups and in the summer of 1966 its chairman, Stokely Carmichael, scared white America with his demand for something called "black power," a cry that blacks all over the country responded to and adopted as their own.

A small leftist publisher read the essay and offered me a contract to develop it into a book. I quickly agreed and in the winter of 1967, in the cold basement of the SNCC office, I wrote *Look Out, Whitey! Black Power's Gon' Get Your Mama.* When it was eventually published in the spring of 1968 it would be the first book to explicate black power and place it in the context of black American history.

The voice I employed in the book was that of an angry young black redefining American history by looking at it through the experiences of those who had suffered that history. The tone of the book was certainly "militant," as many reviewers noted, but it was also filled with much humor, beginning with the title, which white reviewers failed to get. Indeed, a review in the Fort Wayne *News-Sentinel* (July 20, 1968) was headlined: WHITE MAMAS IN DANGER, SAYS BLACK MILITANT, SNCC LESTER. (The review was better than the headline, but I've always thought it safer to avoid Fort Wayne.)

92

When the publisher who asked me to write the book read my manuscript he was, to put it mildly, horrified. The first thing that had to go was the title. Then I had to "do something" about the book's tone. I sat in his office and listened as he detailed what he thought was wrong with the manuscript, the changes I had to make, and how I was to make them.

I didn't know what to do. This was my chance to see my dream of being a published writer come true. Were the changes he wanted me to make *that* important? For all I knew this might be the *only* chance I would ever have to get a book published. But was I so eager to get published that I would turn the manuscript into something that didn't represent what I thought and how I felt? By the time the publisher finished I knew what I had to do. I stood up, stuck out my hand, and asked him for the manuscript. He was surprised, but he gave it to me. When he asked me about returning the advance money, which was only seventy-five dollars, I told him I had spent it. I took the manuscript home and put it in a drawer.

I did not know at the time that was the first of several battles I would have in the coming years over the sound of one of my books. A few editors would fail to understand that for me as a black writer the sound of a book was integral to the content. *Look Out, Whitey!*

would not have been the same book had I rewritten it in a more objective and academic style. The book was not about black power. The book *was* black power!

During the summer of 1967 I acquired an agent, took *Look Out, Whitey!* from the drawer, and gave it to him. The very first publisher he showed it to was Dial Books, James Baldwin's publisher, who accepted the manuscript—title, content, and tone.

My editor was Joyce Johnson, a soft-spoken young woman who would go on to write several memoirs about the Beat Generation and her relationship with Jack Kerouac. I was fortunate to have her as my first editor. The best editor is one who understands what the writer is doing and helps him do it better. That was Joyce.

One late afternoon in the fall of 1967 we finished the final edits and I was preparing to go when Joyce asked, "Have you ever thought about writing children's books?"

I shook my head. "No. Never crossed my mind."

"You have a very simple writing style," she said hesitantly, seemingly not sure if I would take that as a compliment.

"Thank you," I reassured her.

"Would you like to meet the children's book editor?"

I shudder to think what my life would be like if I

had said no. Fortunately, I said yes, remembering what a friend had told me once: "When you have a chance to go somewhere you've never been, get in the car, and after the car is moving, ask, 'Where're we going?'"

Joyce took me to the office of Dial's children's book editor, Phyllis Fogelman. Phyllis was warm and outgoing with a bright smile, and we had an immediate rapport. We chatted for a few minutes and then she asked if I had any ideas for children's books.

I remembered all the notes I had from the slave narratives. "Well, I've been doing research on slavery," I said somewhat timidly, and told her about the Library of Congress slave narrative collection and the books by escaped slaves. "I'd like to do a book on what it was like to be a slave using the words of former slaves."

Her face brightened. "That sounds interesting. Can you write me a one-page description?"

I did so that night and sent it to her. That page became the opening paragraphs of the first chapter of *To Be a Slave*, excluding the prologue.

The voice in which I wrote *To Be a Slave* was an objective one in which I presented historical information about the slave trade, plantation life, the ways slaves resisted slavery, and emancipation. Into this narrative I inserted descriptive passages and stories in the words of the slaves, the objective tone making the rich language and drama of their testi-monies stand out.

One January afternoon in 1969 I received a call from my agent's secretary.

"Julius? Congratulations! *To Be a Slave* has been named a Newbery Honor Book."

"How much money comes with it?" I asked imme-diately.

"Well, none," she said.

"What good is it, then?" I shot back and hung up.

At the time I was living in a housing project on West 26th Street between 9th and 10th Avenues in Manhattan with my first wife, Joan, and our two small children. I had written *To Be a Slave* on a desk in the corner of our living room using an electric typewriter, an amazing innovation I'd bought with part of the advance money from *Look Out, Whitey!*, while the children played on the floor by my chair. Although we were not in danger of starving, the bank account was not in robust health and if the Newbery Honor Award wasn't going to put any money in that account, well, what good was it?

I began to understand that this Newbery thing might be important when I learned that Isaac Bashevis Singer's *When Shlemiel Went to Warsaw and Other Stories* was the only other Newbery Honor Book that year. However, I remained so ignorant of the world of children's literature that years passed before I realized that my first children's book had been accorded the kind of recognition most writers never receive.

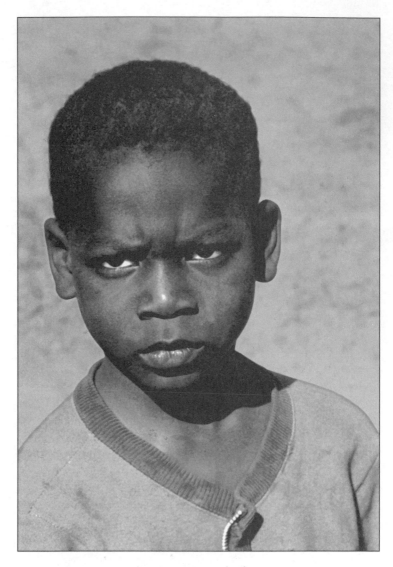

Mississippi, 1966

Sometimes . . . the matter of which I'm writing is too deep or too metaphysical for adults.

Russell Hoban

For more than forty years I have kept a commonplace book in which I copy passages I've underlined in books I'm reading. One of the earliest quotes in it is from Marcus Aurelius: "It loved to happen." I could not have been more than twenty-two when I came across those words in a book during my first year in New York City. I lived on West End Avenue near 79th Street in a tiny one-room whose only window looked into an air shaft. I worked in a bookstore at 57th Street and 5th Avenue operated by the now-defunct publisher Doubleday. Each day after work I returned to my dismal one-room around six, slept until nine, then got up and wrote and/or read until one or two, then slept until seven-thirty, when it was time to go to work.

On one of those nights I read the simple sentence of the Roman philosopher: "It loved to happen." I did not understand who or what the "It" was, but the words crystallized something essential about how I had been living my life and how I would continue to live it.

I did not then, nor do I now, make major decisions. I wait for the "It" to happen—lovingly. I can best describe the "It" as a calm, inner clarity whose judgment I accept without question. Thus it had been when I recognized that my way would be through writing, not music or art. So it was with learning that writing for children as well as adults would benefit me in ways writing for either alone might not.

In the early 1970s Phyllis invited me to attend an American Library Association (ALA) convention in Chicago, where I signed books. What I remember most, however, were the hours I spent wandering through the vast convention hall where publishers had their display booths. Librarians and teachers were there from all over the country and most of them carried shopping bags, sometimes two, filled with books. The expressions on some of their faces were akin to lust, so passionate was their love for books.

I had never been around so many people for whom bringing children and books together was tantamount to a religious calling. How many children had become lifelong readers simply because of the passion of a librarian for books? At that first ALA convention I learned that I had something in common with librarians and children—we read in order to be moved, and even changed by what we read.

Librarians and children read as if books matter. Kafka wrote that "a book should serve as the axe for the frozen sea within us," and Hannah Arendt described the "poet's task" as "coin[ing] the words we live by." This was how I had always read but many of my teachers, especially in high school, had thought it more important to analyze the themes and imagery in poems and novels. They approached literature as if it were a cipher to be decoded, which may be why most Americans do not read anything serious after they finish high school and regard literature as an assignment they will fail because they won't understand the symbols.

When I taught literature I began each book by asking, "What was your response to the book? Did you like it? Not like it? Why? Why not?" The students would look at me as if they didn't understand. No teacher, they told me, had ever asked them for their personal response to a book. I was always saddened by this. I did not write to be analyzed, and perhaps that was one reason why I enjoyed writing for children. They were open to letting a book be an axe to shatter "the frozen sea within." At that first ALA convention I attended I discovered that librarians were people who were not afraid of the axe.

As I met more and more children's book writers, I

learned that their attitudes toward books did not differ from that of the librarians. People read each other's work and appreciated it; they were genuinely pleased when someone's book was successful. I wonder if something in the nature of writing for children helps us maintain a perspective on ourselves as writers. Our ultimate judges are not critics but children who care only that we open our hearts to them, something few adults do—for children or each other.

Martin Buber wrote that "all real living is meeting," and that "true community" arises when people live in "mutual relation with one another." Mutual relation is not possible if one regards a child as an "It" and not a "Thou." Unfortunately, regarding children as "Its" is more the norm, one I experience when someone asks me, "When are you going to write a *real* book?" as if children are not "real" people.

Many believe that writing for children is so easy anybody can do it because children are Lockean blank slates waiting eagerly to be written upon by all-knowing and wise adults. In this post–J. K. Rowling/ Harry Potter world, a parade of celebrities and established fiction authors have taken to writing for children, generally picture books. With few exceptions the books are moralistic, didactic, poorly conceived and poorly written, none of which keeps them from selling, and sometimes selling quite well.

We relate to children as "Its" when we forget what it was like to be a child. Childhood is a time of extraordinary complexity during which we undergo monumental changes in an amazingly brief period of time. This is especially true during that critical period from sixth grade through high school, ages twelve to eighteen, when we undergo more major changes than at any comparable period of our lives. We enter love relationships, and in this encounter with another we also come into a new awareness of ourselves. Some of us even meet the person with whom we will spend the rest of our lives, or think we want to. We do a lot of thinking about who we are and where we fit in the world and start trying to make a cohesive whole of the many facets of our identities—racial, religious, gender, as well as those attributes unique to our personalities. We begin the process of defining our values. As children we believed and espoused the beliefs of our parents, teachers, and religious leaders. During adolescence we test those values against our experiences and begin to shape the ideals and concepts that will enable us to determine what we consider ethical and unethical.

Most of us want to live our lives in such a way that we do as little harm as possible to ourselves and others. That sounds simple. In reality, it is quite difficult. And unless we begin that journey during adolescence, our lives will have less meaning than they could have.

One of the reasons I write for children is because the questions of identity that are central to childhood, especially adolescence, remain ones of pressing urgency for me, even at age sixty-five. I certainly know more about who I am now than I did when I was fourteen. However, as I look back over the expanse of a lifetime I wonder often what might have been had I made that choice and not another, and there is the pain of deep regret at opportunities missed and risks not taken. All I didn't do has shaped my identity as surely as the opportunities grasped and risks taken.

Today my identity is molded by the inescapable fact that the sum of my past is greater than the sum of my future. When I was young I asked myself only: What do I want to do? When I became a husband and a father what I wanted to do had to be balanced by the needs of my family. Now there is no longer time to do all I would like to do, or even all I need to do. There is only time to do that which is most vital for my soul's odyssey.

My books, all of them, have risen from the need to know who I am. Answering questions about my slave ancestors in *To Be a Slave, Long Journey Home, This Strange New Feeling,* and my other books retelling folktales represented responses to the racial aspect of my identity. More personal explorations into other facets of my identity are found in such books as *Othello: A Novel* (Scholastic, 1995), a novelization of the Shakespeare play; *Pharaoh's Daughter* (Harcourt/Silver Whistle, 2000), a novel about the childhood of Moses in ancient Egypt; and *Ackamarackus* (Scholastic, 2002), a book of silly fables.

Writing for children was a choice to remain in close relationship to the mystery of identity, a choice I made when I was still a child. In church one Sunday morning a baby started crying while Daddy was preaching. Practically the entire congregation looked around to see where the crying was coming from. Daddy shouted, "What're you looking at? Didn't you cry when you were a baby?"

Within all of us, there is still that baby who cried, that baby who cries. By deciding to write for children, I chose to continue listening to that crying child.

Playground, New York City, 1966

With tales you can rouse people from their sleep.

Rebbe Nachman of Bratslav

Traditionally folktales taught the adults and children of a group how to live, what kinds of behavior to emulate, and what kinds to avoid so they could be reasonably assured of having a life approved of by the deities. Folktales recorded the psychic history of a group by evoking the past, affirming the present, and showing the way to the future.

Such tales did not have individual authors. Though they may have been created by especially gifted people within the group, tales were only passed from one generation to the next because they fulfilled a need of the group. Today the oral tradition has been replaced by mass media and children's books have become the conservators of the oral tradition.

This is, of course, a paradox. Stories from the oral tradition cease to be oral once they are written down. When confined to the page they become literature, the product of a single mind, one person's skill with words and silence. Traditional stories, however, come from a community and are shaped and reshaped by all who tell them and hear them. Literature exists on the page where it cannot be changed. Stories are elastic and are created anew on the tongue of each teller.

The nature of our society is inimical to storytelling because we no longer live in cohesive communities. We no longer educate each other with stories in which our joys and sorrows are refashioned into an art that serves as a mirror for the entire community. The question becomes then: How can one fit the marvelous elasticity of a story onto the page without injuring the story? It is possible only if one refuses to regard the page as the story's final destination, an exalted end. The page is merely the means to return stories to the mouths and tongues of anyone who wishes to tell them.

Generally, when rewritten for books, stories from the oral tradition are presented in a disembodied voice. The story is written but it is not *told*. A story can be *told* only by a person. When the story is being presented by someone called an author, the author writes words because that is what authors do. However, a storyteller *uses* the book as a vehicle for his or her voice and personality.

The idea for me to retell the Uncle Remus stories came from the late Augusta Baker, then head of children's services of the New York Library system. She had read my first books of retellings, *Black Folktales* (Richard Baron, 1968) and *The Knee-High Man* (Dial Books, 1972). She asked Phyllis Fogelman if she thought I would be interested in retelling the Uncle Remus stories. When Phyllis called and presented the idea, I wondered why I hadn't thought of it. If there was ever a project I was born to do, it was this one.

When I began, I wanted to do what Joel Chandler Harris had done, namely, write tales so that readers (listeners) would feel as if they were being spoken to and invited into a relationship in which the story was not separate from the teller, in which story and teller were one so that listener and story became one. I wanted the listener to be transformed from solitary individual and become humanity.

However, a number of issues had to be resolved. The first was who was Joel Chandler Harris? His Uncle Remus had become a symbol of the stereotypical subservient slave, someone who preferred slavery and paternalism to freedom. I needed to know if Harris had set out to create a figure demeaning to blacks.

The biographies I read convinced me that far from intending to demean blacks, Harris had sought to honor three slaves from whom he had heard many of the stories and who had been like surrogate fathers to him, an orphan. The character of Uncle Remus was a melding of these three men. Even though Harris's Uncle Remus would now be considered an "Uncle Tom," I recognized that only the politically conservative slaves would have made the effort to remember the tales. The memories of such slaves deserved to be respected and honored alongside the memories of the Nat Turners. All had their places in the grand design.

The next issue was the tales themselves. How authentic were they? How much of the tales was African-American and how much Harris? The evidence indicated that Harris was scrupulous in that he collected many versions of a single story to satisfy himself of its authenticity. His diligent work resulted in the single largest collection of African-American tales from slavery.

My research made me feel close to Harris when I learned he was a painfully shy man who stuttered. However, when Harris adopted the persona of Uncle Remus and told tales in dialect, his stutter vanished. I am also very shy and I stuttered terribly as a child, something to which I am still prone at unpredictable moments, but something I never do when I sing, in English or Hebrew.

I knew that retelling the Uncle Remus tales was risky. Blacks might hate me for resurrecting a figure they considered shameful, and perhaps many whites who had grown up with the stories would hate me for daring to presume that I could or should do anything with them.

As I read them it was clear that these were good stories. But the dialects made them almost unintelligible and the figure of Uncle Remus as portrayed by Harris was unacceptable for contemporary readers. But these were not reasons to reject an important part of black heritage. Could I preserve the tales and still honor the southern, black oral tradition from which they had come? Should I keep Uncle Remus or create another storyteller? Should I change the setting to, say, a barbershop in Harlem, or a stoop or porch in a black neighborhood? I decided such approaches would distract from what was important, the stories. Everything else was secondary to placing the stories in the hearts of a new generation.

I decided that the personality of my storyteller would be communicated entirely through voice, through his asides, imagery, and allusions. I trusted voice, not only because of the voices I had heard in childhood, but I grew up during the "golden age of radio" and had a live radio show for eight years on WBAI-FM in New York. I knew the power of voice and all that could be conveyed by it. I wanted to re-create on paper the sound and feeling of what it was like to sit on that porch in Pine Bluff late at night, what it had been like to sit on the floor in the living room in front of the big Philco radio and hear a deep voice intone: "Who knows what evil lurks in the hearts of men? The Shadow knows."

What I would have to sacrifice, however, was the richness of the storytellers who populated Harris's tales, as well as the range of storytelling voices. Some of the tales were told by African Jack, who spoke Gullah, a black dialect spoken on the Georgia and South Carolina Sea Islands. There were also women storytellers whose voices I sacrificed. In the way Harris presented the tales he sought to re-create life on the plantation, relationships between slaves, and between slaves and whites. I considered doing the same, but without Harris's nostalgia. Eventually I decided doing so would distract from the tales, which, to me, was what was important.

Having decided that my storyteller would be a voice, a presence who would not be seen, the next problem was the language. I decided on a mixture of northern and southern black speech, a language similar to that I used in *Black Folktales*. And, as I had in *Black Folktales*, I knew my storyteller would make reference to things of the contemporary world. For some Harris purists that would be unacceptable, but folktales are not historical artifacts. I was not interested in preserving Harris's work. I wanted to offer the tales to a new audience in a new century.

The tales are filled with words that are archaic now. Only because of my southern roots did I understand that when Uncle Remus says "branch," he is not referring to a tree but a creek. (Up north people drink bourbon and water. Down south they drink bourbon and branch.) The stories as Harris told them are rooted in time, and the stories as I told them had to be also if they were to be believed.

The final decision was how to order the stories. Harris had published them randomly. I decided to bring together all the stories in which Brer Rabbit was the principal character and these comprise the first two volumes. In the third volume other animals were the primary characters, while the last volume was primarily ghost and witch tales and miscellaneous stories. However, the character of Brer Rabbit is pervasive and he appears in all four volumes, sometimes in a supporting role, sometimes as the focus.

Working on the tales led me to a new understanding of Brer Rabbit as trickster, and consequently to a deeper understanding of myself. Some scholars interpret the Uncle Remus tales as a socio-political document that chronicles black resistance to slavery—the weak and wily triumphing over the powerful, etc., etc. But trickster tales are universal and cannot be explained in every culture on the basis of such a socio-political analysis.

As I wrote in the introduction to the second volume, *More Tales of Uncle Remus,* a primary characteristic of the trickster tale is the absence of morality. Uncle Remus said, "Creatures don't know nothing at all about that's good and that's bad. They don't know right from wrong. They see what they want and they get it if they can, by hook or crook." The moralist may be outraged and offended by Brer Rabbit or any trickster because trickster lies, cheats, deceives, and is seldom caught and never really pays for the chaos he causes. Roger Abrahams, the eminent scholar of Afro-American folklore, wrote that we can only enter trickster tales by suspending "moral conscience." It is precisely in this suspension of moral conscience that Trickster becomes the avatar of a higher morality.

Those who interpret the Brer Rabbit tales from a socio-political perspective point to the ingenious ways Brer Rabbit escapes the lethal plots of Brer Wolf and Brer Fox, who, in such an analysis, represent white people. But Brer Rabbit is not always the victim. He is as often the instigator of trouble, violence, and even murder. Trickster is beyond such a simplistic dichotomy, either pole of which would merely make him a cute little bunny.

The outcome of trickster tales is not as crucial as

the spirit of the trickster, which attracts and repels us simultaneously. Roger Abrahams points out that "Trickster's vitality and inventiveness are valued for their own sake. The principle of vitality seems more important than that of right or wrong." What we value in Trickster is not only the amorality, but also the raw energy of Life and Nature he shows us and allows us to experience.

But there is another level to the meaning of the trickster. That is what Abrahams calls "patterned disordering." This is not a disordering that leads to chaos and destruction. Quite the contrary. It is disorder integral to the ordered pattern of life without which we become rigid and sterile. It is Trickster in us who knocks over the glass of water at a dinner party that threatens to be pretentious and stuffy. It is Trickster who makes so-called Freudian slips, who laughs at inappropriate times. Trickster is the class clown, the child or student who has a genius for knowing how to walk a line between fun and trouble, the child who is disruptive without being rebellious. And this child is always entertaining because Trickster is charming and likeable, surrounded as he is by an aura of innocence and vulnerability.

The philologist Káoly Kerényi wrote that "in mythology, we hear the world telling its own story to itself." That is why we love Brer Rabbit. Through him we hear a portion of our story. It is not a story we could hear in any other way, perhaps because Trickster's amorality shames us as we witness him telling preposterous lies and getting away with them. But, Kerényi writes, "shameless untruthfulness is a property of the world." Because we are human such "shameless" lying belongs to each of us, loath may we be to admit it. Through trickster tales we live with, laugh with, and love something of ourselves that is beyond our powers to redeem.

Trickster keeps us in reality. And this is where Trickster's amoral morality is superior to our moral posturing, our certitude that we know, absolutely, what is right and what is wrong. The more we are alienated from Trickster, the more likely we are to believe the inflated ideas we have about ourselves. Many of the Brer Rabbit stories turn on the fact that he exploits the other animals' images of themselves. He appeals to their vanity, their pride, their posturing egos, and invariably they believe him. The instant they do, they are in Brer Rabbit's power and lost to themselves.

Trickster's function is to keep Order from taking itself too seriously. In Kerényi's words, "Disorder belongs to the totality of life, and the spirit of this disorder is the trickster. His function is to add disorder to order and so make a whole, to render possible, within the fixed bounds of what is permitted, an experience of what is not permitted."

That is the charisma of Brer Rabbit. Through him we experience "what is not permitted," and thereby we are made whole. Not perfect, but whole. And to be whole is to love our irredeemable imperfections with the same passion we love our virtues.

Where others find it logical that the Brer Rabbit tales were told during slavery, I find it remarkable. The tales were not mere psychological compensation for the lack of power in the slaves' lives. Rather, they represented an extraordinary effort to balance the totalitarian order of the slave system with archetypal disorder and thereby create psychic wholeness.

Isn't it remarkable that these animal tales created by slaves speak so directly and with such clarity to us who live in conditions far removed from slavery? In these tales created by slaves is one of the vital voices of our humanity.

The first two volumes were written at the same time on an amazing technological marvel called a computer. No longer would I have to spend a month typing the final draft of a manuscript, nor be concerned about using carbon paper to make onionskin copies. Gone forever was the laborious process of correcting mistakes by lining up the typewriter carriage with the offending letter, and then taking a piece of tape with chalk on one side and putting it between the paper and the ribbon, and by typing the wrong letter, erase it, and then backspace and put in the correct one. But the computer had one disadvantage: Being neurotically compulsive about rewriting, I could and do rewrite far more than I did before.

Phyllis Fogelman was not my editor on the first two volumes of the Uncle Remus tales and I don't remember now why she assigned a new, young editor to me. Neither do I recall that editor's name or even what she looked like, but I remember vividly the editorial conference we had in her small office.

Because I rewrite compulsively my manuscripts do not require major editing. When editors have good suggestions for changes in wording, or pose questions whose answers will make the manuscript stronger, I readily take them. And I always welcome help with punctuation, the rules of which are as mysterious to me as quantum mechanics.

Unfortunately, my new editor did not confine herself to commas and colons. She went immediately for the heart of the manuscript with her objections to the contemporary references, the occasional changes in verb tense from past to present and past again, sometimes in the same paragraph, and she really didn't like what she considered to be "sexism" in some of the stories. She especially hated this passage.

In "Brer Rabbit and the Mosquitoes," Brer Rabbit is courting Brer Wolf's daughter.

> Brer Wolf's daughter who had always thought Brer Rabbit was kind of cute, put on her mascara and eyeliner and whatever else it is that the women put on their face. She squeezed herself into a pair of jeans four sizes too small. Have mercy! And she put on a pink halter top! When Brer Rabbit saw her, he thought he'd died and gone to heaven.

I didn't see what was wrong with my Uncle Remus describing a woman as wearing a halter top since many women did, in fact, wear halter tops. Perhaps none did in my editor's social circuit but in Uncle Remus's neighborhood, have mercy! (My editor should have been happy I hadn't described Brer Wolf's daughter's cleavage.) I was not going to rewrite history and culture to satisfy white feminism or a white version of social reality.

The editor went through the manuscript page by page and I patiently and repeatedly explained why I used the language and allusions I did. I saw nothing incongruous with God reading *TV Guide,* but that was because I had grown up in a culture in which God did all kinds of things that had not made their way into the Bible and maybe should have.

She continued to argue with me as if it were her book. It wasn't. Neither was it mine. These stories had come from the lives of black people and my responsibility was to them. I did understand her concern that the contemporary references would make the book outdated. Italo Calvino's *Italian Folktales* had recently been published and she used it as an example of the kind of cultural neutrality she thought my book should be.

But folktales exist in time, and Harris's use of allusions contemporary to his time did not injure the stories, but added and preserved details of the minutia of that era's daily life.

In "Brer Rabbit Finally Gets Beaten," my editor didn't like the following paragraph:

> Brer Rabbit went into training. He bought a red jogging suit, a green sweatband, and some yellow Adidas sneakers, and he jogged ten miles every day. Then he'd come home and do a whole mess of push-ups, sit-ups, and skip rope to his records. Some folks wondered if he was training for a race or "Soul Train."

She wanted to delete "Soul Train." To do so would've taken away the humor and the narrator's voice. The story resided as much in the voice as the plots which scarcely varied. It is the voice of the storyteller, the colorful details, and nuances of language the teller uses which maintain our interest as readers (listeners).

The heart of storytelling is the human encounter between teller and listener. The goal of the teller is to make the listener more alive to him- or herself. Especially in tales from the oral tradition, it is the voice of the teller which softens and humanizes the horrors and violence with which the tales abound.

My editor did not think the voice and inconsistencies in grammatical usage would communicate to white readers. They weren't supposed to, I told her. But where was the harm in asking whites to read stories written in a black vernacular? That's what Harris had done. The stories would communicate to anyone. That the language carried nuances and evoked memories that would be available primarily to blacks merely gave the stories an added dimension.

For her, folktales were historical artifacts. For me, they are a breathing, pulsating reality that are in no way incompatible with shopping malls and halter tops. My Uncle Remus was as much a man of his time as his predecessor was of his. In the voices of both are the presences of all black people whose lives shaped the tales, whose lives were shaped by the tales. My Uncle Remus speaks in a collective voice, which is why it moves backward and forward in time so easily, referring at one moment to "the haslett" and at the next to Adidas sneakers. It is a voice which stands simultaneously outside history while being at the heart of history.

To have told the stories with any other voice was to think stories existed apart from their telling. They cannot because, ultimately, the stories are about our lives, all of us. If this were not so, these stories created by slaves would not be the source of joy they are and have been for whites and blacks.

That is the paradox: The universality of the stories is only revealed if the voice in the stories is specific. The way to the universal is through the particular.

Uncle Remus would've said to my editor:

Lord, chile, how come you worrying so much about how I tell these stories? Ain't nothing that ever come out of my mouth ever done nobody no harm. Leastways not when I done brushed my teeth good and jiggled Listerine around in my mouth. That stuff tastes worser than hog's breath and don't come asking me how I know what hog's breath tastes like. That ain't none of your business. Now, as I was saying, don't you be trying to put these stories in a book without using my voice. Folks done tried that and you know what happened? Them stories had to go to the hospital. That's the truth! Them stories had to have highway bypass operations. Then they had to have "bad" grammar transplanted into them and take all kinds of pills to keep 'em from getting infections from literature. Then they had to take baths every day for about forty-eleven months. So, you leave these stories be. They don't be needing no clean clothes or grease for their hair and please don't come shining they shoes. What you got to understand is that the story is me. If you can't accept the story the way it rides on my voice that mean you can't accept me.

Voice is who I am.

Voice is who you are.

If I listen deeply to your voice, I am the recipient of a wonderful and irreplaceable gift—you.

If you listen deeply to mine, you will receive something equally rare and precious—me.

Santiago, Cuba, 1967

The artist must penetrate into the world, feel the fate of human beings, of peoples, with real love. There is no art for art's sake. One must be interested in the entire realm of life.

Marc Chagall

Many writers retell folktales from cultures other than their own. I do not. In *How Many Spots Does a Leopard Have? And Other Tales* (Scholastic, 1989), I retold African and Jewish stories, but did not feel the same ease retelling them as I did tales from the black South.

Many years ago I objected strongly to those who played music or told stories from traditions other than their own. My first published article was an attack in *Sing Out!* on young white folk musicians who were trying to play guitar and sing like black Mississippi bluesmen. This was in the mid-1960s, a time when blacks viewed any white encroachment on what we considered "our culture" a declaration of cultural warfare. Two experiences changed my mind about who "owns" culture.

Some years ago when I taught in the Afro-American Studies department at the University of

Massachusetts, I noticed on the first day of class that a white student was answering, and answering correctly, every question I asked. With her light brown hair and blue eyes she looked more like the stereotypical cheerleader than someone who would know any-thing about the literature of the Harlem Renaissance. However, as the semester progressed her responses to questions as well as the kinds of questions she asked indicated a knowledge of black culture that went beyond what she could have gathered from reading alone. Her grasp of black literature and culture was not merely intellectual; it was visceral.

At that time I thought one had to be black to *really* understand black literature and culture, but here was Cynthia Packard, from a small town in western Massa-chusetts, who, I would learn, never saw a black person until she was eight years old and did not have much contact with blacks until college. She went on to major in Afro-American Studies and later, on my recommen-dation, was hired to teach in the department.

Second experience: During my days as a folk singer my repertoire consisted of original songs and blues, work songs and what we then called Negro spirituals. Although I sang with passion and feeling, black audiences did not respond to me as emotion-ally as they did to other black singers. I was a minister's son and had grown up in the church, but something was missing from my singing of black music.

I converted to Judaism in 1982. Traditionally, the Jewish worship service is led by the cantor, not the rabbi, because the service is conducted almost exclusively in song. However, in Judaism a knowledgeable layperson can do anything in a service an ordained rabbi or cantor can. Because of my love of Jewish music and the encouragement of Rabbi Ed Friedman, the rabbi then of Congregation B'nai Israel, the Conservative synagogue in Northampton, Massachusetts, to which I belonged, I began leading parts of the service and eventually became cantor for the High Holidays. This is a position of such centrality to the Rosh Hashanah and Yom Kippur services that the service leader is given a special title—*schliach tzibbur*—messenger of the congregation.

Two highlights of the Rosh Hashanah and Yom Kippur services are the "Hineni" prayer sung on Rosh Hashanah and Yom Kippur and the Kol Nidre prayer, which begins Yom Kippur. "Hineni"—Here Am I—is a very dramatic prayer in which the *schliach tzibbur* starts singing at the back of the congregation and continues singing as he walks slowly down the aisle and onto the pulpit, or *bimah* as it is called in Hebrew. In the prayer the *schliach tzibbur* says he is unworthy to pray on behalf of the congregation and asks God to accept his prayers on their behalf even though he is more lowly than a worm, among other things.

As Rosh Hashanah drew near that first year I was to be *schliach tzibbur*, my nervousness and fear accelerated into terror. "Worm" did not begin to describe what I felt like. What did I think I was doing? I was black; the Jews of the congregation had heard these prayers sung since before they could remember. Who was I to think I could pray on their behalf? But I tried.

I was amazed when some members of the congregation told me that my singing had taken them back to when they were children and had attended High Holy Day services with their grandparents. Holocaust survivors said, with tears in their eyes, that they had not been so moved by singing in synagogue since before the war. Israelis wanted to know how long I had lived in Israel because my Hebrew pronunciation was so good.

How was it possible that I, the black son and grandson of southern ministers, who never got more than a polite response when singing Negro spirituals, brought tears to the eyes of Jews in their seventies and eighties when singing ancient prayers in Hebrew, a language in which I was not fluent?

The soul's identity does not necessarily correspond to the race, culture, class, or nation into which one is born. One of the sins of the last part of the twentieth century was the increasing insistence by more and more people that race and ethnicity corresponded to personal identity and supplanted it. Such a formulation unknowingly dressed white supremacy in new racial clothing. Just as whites used to believe (and some still do) that blacks by virtue of being black were incapable of, in the words of Thomas Jefferson, "a thought above the level of plain narration," and were "inferior to the whites in the endowments both of body and mind," there arose a generation of blacks who maintained that whites were incapable of understanding black culture, a generation of women who argued that men could not write female characters as well as women. They are as wrong as Jefferson was.

But we live at a time when ethnic and cultural differences have been inflated to such an extent that our emphasis on what we do not have in common all too often overrides our common sense. I do not mean to minimize cultural differences, nor imply that all cultural differences can be understood and bridged. That is not so. But to ascribe values to our differences to the detriment of our humanity is sinful.

To equate identity with race and culture is to deny

the power of the imagination which can be the empathic bridge between nations, cultures, and individuals. Instead of placing barriers around a culture and denying others permission to enter, we should be thankful that people from outside our group are interested, curious, want to learn, want to feel a sense of belonging with us. Cultures are not private reserves but humble offerings.

Even though most of the books I've written have their roots in black culture, I do not write only for black people. I write for anyone who honors my efforts by picking up a book I've written because, in its essence, story is one heart touching another. Story is the vehicle we ride as we set out to explore the infinite inner space of our beings.

As a writer I am responsible to the story as an expression of the heart's drama. Through story we bridge that loneliness intrinsic to being human, and in so doing we touch our common humanity. The simple and incontrovertible fact is that we all grieve those who left our lives before we wanted them to, as others will grieve us for leaving before they want us to. If I learned nothing else standing before those open caskets in my father's church, it was that death makes us equals.

For writers the issue is not whether we write

about our culture or someone else's. The issue is what it has always been—that we write well, that we write with integrity, that we write as much of the truth as we are able to apprehend.

Sharecropper's family, Mississippi, 1966

No story comes from nowhere; new stories are born from old—it is the new combinations that make them new.

Salman Rushdie

One of the most common questions asked of writers is "Where do you get your ideas?" Each book's inception is different. However, whatever the book, it is not born from an idea but from the writer's *feelings* about the idea. I write about what is important in the biography of my emotional life.

From the moment my father told me our family history began with a bill of a sale, to that hot July day at the edge of a field in Laurel, Mississippi, when I wondered what it had been like to be a slave, and into the early nineties, re-creating the experiences of slaves and the culture they created had been of vital importance to me. This was a common denominator among the books of historical fiction (*Long Journey Home; This Strange New Feeling; Black Cowboy, Wild Horses*), the retellings of folktales (*Black Folktales, The Knee-High Man, The Complete Tales of Uncle Remus, How Many Spots*

Does a Leopard Have?, John Henry) and my first novel for adults *(Do Lord Remember Me).* Even though writing these books engaged me emotionally, I never thought of them as personal books. These were books that something, or perhaps someone, inside compelled me to write.

I return, yet again, to that child standing before the open caskets in his father's church trying to will life into the dead. I was certainly not aware of making a conscious decision to offer a portion of my life to the dead. But apparently they took my standing before their coffins, my walks in cemeteries, as invitations to re-enter the realm of the living through me.

Until recently I could sense a long line of dead slaves inside me, waiting patiently for me to tell their stories. Our lives begin generations, centuries maybe, before we are born and the personal pronoun "I" is not sufficient to describe our totality. That "I" consists, at a minimum, of the personal "I" we project into the world. But there is another "I," the ancestral "I," which is comprised of all those generations needed to create us. So, when I say that the books I wrote from *Look Out, Whitey!* to *John Henry* were not "personal books," I mean they were books written by the ancestral "I," the black and Jewish ones. They were expressions of grieving, my attempts to bring life to the dead. I would never cease writing from the ancestral "I" but in the early 1990s the personal "I" began seeking expression, though I was not aware of this at the time.

I had signed a contract with Scholastic to retell some of the great love stories of Western civilization— *Romeo and Juliet, Tristan and Isolde, Eros and Psyche,* among others. Retellings were easy for me because once I established voice, my responsibility was to be faithful to the story lines and characterizations of the original tales. However, being faithful to the originals meant neglecting a more personal voice. That was about to change.

When I started researching the book, Shakespeare's *Othello* was one of the first tales I encountered. I was probably thirteen when I saw the play on television. Though I had started reading Shakespeare by then I had not yet read *Othello.* I remember sitting before the television, rapt. As the ending unfolded and I sensed Othello was going to kill Desdemona, everything in me was screaming at him, *No! No! Don't!* When he finally did, I was numb with disbelief. A part of me still is.

I had begun with one idea—a book retelling the great love stories of Western civilization—but writing a novel based on Shakespeare's *Othello* engaged me emotionally. I *cared* about Othello and Desdemona. Not only because of how deeply I had been affected when I saw the play on television, but also because of my family history. Adolph stepped across racial and religious lines to create a family with Maggie. My mother ignored the protests of her aunt Rena to marry my black-skinned father. And I could not ignore the interracial love relationships in my life.

I am presently married for the third (and last!) time. My wife is white, as were my previous wives. Many blacks view this as irrefutable proof that I deserve to be Exhibit A in the Hall of Black Racial Self-hatred. I suppose there is a certain logic to this if one makes race the core of being and exchanges the risks of personal identity for the security of a collective one. I never did. My sophomore year at Fisk I was president of the Philosophy Club, and at one of our meetings I and one of the deans were on a panel to discuss "Individuality vs. Conformity." I do not recall what I said that prompted Dean Simpson, I will call her, to turn to me and say, "Mr. Lester, you must learn to conform." I shot back, "I will not." "You must," she countered, her voice rising. "I will not," I said louder, and the panel discussion ended with the dean and I yelling back and forth repeatedly, "You must conform!" "I will not!" Since childhood my understanding of what it was to be *someBODY* meant never allowing someone else to determine your identity.

All writing is autobiographical if one understands that the subject matter is the writer's emotions, ancestral and/or personal. In writing about Othello and Desdomona I would be exploring an aspect of the emotional lives and loves of my great-grandparents, my parents and myself.

During this same period (circa 1991 to 1995) I also wrote *And All Our Wounds Forgiven* (Arcade, 1994), which was a finalist for the National Book Critics Circle Award. It was a novel about a civil rights leader of the 1960s and his white lover. I can't recall whether *Othello: A Novel* (Scholastic, 1996) or *And All Our Wounds Forgiven* was written first. They were published two years apart, but dates of publication are not accurate gauges of the actual writing. Both novels focused on interracial relationships and the tension between the social and political identity imposed because of race and that identity one seeks to live for him- or herself.

I had lived with such a tension since adolescence, though I could have resolved it easily at any time. Many years ago, a close, black male friend saw me with a black woman, and assumed I was romantically involved with her. He pulled me aside and asked, "Are you thinking about leaving your wife?" I didn't understand him at first and, puzzled, wanted to know why I would do that. A little befuddled, he stammered, "Well, brother, she's white." My response was immediate: "Since I didn't marry her because she was white, I won't be leaving her because she's white." (There was a black professor at a major university who, during a period when he was being pressured by black students about his white wife, began each term's first classes by announcing, "I will not be leaving my wife this semester.")

I was hurt when a black student told me that black students at the University of Massachusetts boycotted my courses because my wife was white. It hurt when I learned there were blacks who refused to read anything I wrote because of my wife's race, or because I was a Jew. It hurt when blacks would tell me I was no longer black because I had converted to Judaism. But these hurts were nothing compared to the hurt I would have inflicted on myself if I had given others the power to dictate whom I could and could not love, and how I could and could not worship God.

The writing of *And All Our Wounds Forgiven* and *Othello: A Novel* helped broaden my view of myself as a writer. I would always be an interpreter for the dead, but now I needed to meld the ancestral and personal. This occurred when I undertook retelling *Little Black Sambo.*

There is nothing overtly Jewish about *Sam and the Tigers* (Dial Books for Young Readers, 1996), the title of my version of *Little Black Sambo.* But, for me it is in part a Jewish book because I approached the writing as if I were writing midrash, a Jewish way of looking at a text which requires one to bring his imagination to bear on the text. Earlier in this book I wondered who in the Torah had the task of remembering Joseph's bones. Midrash begins with questions about a text. In the story of Cain and Abel, there are these lines: "And Cain spoke to Abel his brother. And it came to pass, when they were in the field, that Cain rose up against Abel his brother, and killed him." (Genesis 4:8) The Torah does not tell us what Cain said to Abel, or how the two brothers happened to be in the field together. The Torah doesn't consider such details important for the story it is telling. Or perhaps the Torah deliberately omits details so as to invite our imaginations into the text. Through studying and teaching midrash I slowly gained the confidence to use traditional tales as starting places for stories of my own.

The idea to retell *Little Black Sambo* came from my participation in discussions on two Internet lists: alt.rec.books.children and Child-Lit, where people debated if the book was racist. Those who'd had the book read to them as children and not seen the illustrations felt it was not, while those who had seen the illustrations thought it was. Almost everyone, however, expressed affection for the story.

During one of those discussions someone wrote that Jerry Pinkney was doing a new version of it. I called Jerry, miffed that he hadn't talked to me about writing the text.

He chuckled and said, "I mentioned at a conference that maybe the time was ripe for *somebody* to do a new version."

I said, "Why don't we do it?"

There was a long pause on the other end of the phone. "Are you serious?" he wanted to know.

"Sure. Why not?"

There was another long pause.

"Why don't I call Phyllis and see what she thinks," I put in.

When I told Phyllis that Jerry and I were talking about doing a new version of *Little Black Sambo,* I was met with another long pause at the other end of the phone. Finally she said, "If anybody except you and Jerry had called up with that idea I would've said you're crazy."

Her response was a compliment to the close working and personal relationship Jerry and I had developed. He had illustrated the Uncle Remus books but we became friends while working on *John Henry,* a book that had been his idea. He'd had Phyllis ask me if I would be interested in doing the text. I knew "John Henry" from my days as a folk singer, but it was not one of my favorite songs. But I didn't want to turn down the chance of doing another book with Jerry, so I told Phyllis that I wanted to talk with him about it.

Publishers do not like writers and artists to talk to each other. Perhaps they've had too many bad experiences of writers trying to tell artists what to illustrate and how the illustrations should look. Because of my background in art and because I didn't trust white publishers to always know how to evaluate depictions of blacks, I insisted on having a clause in my contracts requiring publishers to include me in the decision of who the illustrators of my books would be as well as letting me see the art before the final paintings were done. Among the eight artists who've illustrated books of mine, Jerry is the only one with whom I have had a collaborative relationship.

It began with our initial phone conversation about John Henry. Jerry talked about his father as being "my John Henry," a man who overcame the odds and did so with dignity. As I listened I began to understand why doing this book was important for Jerry, but nothing he was saying made *me* care about John Henry.

And there was a problem. The story ends with John Henry's death. How could I make his death acceptable for small children?

I don't recall what it was Jerry said, but suddenly the image of Martin Luther King, Jr., and his death came to me. I remembered a story I'd heard from

Reverend Will Campbell, a friend and white southern Baptist minister who had been active in the civil rights movement. He had officiated at the funeral of a woman who had died young, but who had led an extraordinary life in her less than thirty years. At the end of his eulogy Will asked everyone to stand and applaud her for a life well lived. I told Jerry I'd do the text.

Death. I was still standing before the open coffins trying to feel what it was like to be dead and trying to replace death with life. What made writing *John Henry* matter for me was not re-creating the story of a black folk hero. I wrote the story for all the children whose mothers or fathers had died and the lifetime of grieving that lay ahead of them. John Henry's death would remind them of the parent they no longer had, but I wanted them to hear the applause for John Henry as applause, too, for the parent they no longer had. I wanted the tears in their eyes to glisten also from a smile on their lips.

Writing *John Henry* was harder than I had anticipated. The text couldn't be more than six to eight pages, which meant I could not use the leisurely exposition and storytelling pace I was accustomed to. I could not explain; I could not use interior monologues to explore the character's emotional life. The story had to move from incident to incident.

I don't recall how many drafts I wrote, but there

were many. Finally I had a text that both Phyllis and Jerry liked. I thought my part in the book was finished. One day I got a call from Jerry, who, in his gentle way, asked, "Can you cut something on page four? I need more space." I didn't understand, but I respected him and cut the number of lines he said he needed. Even after the book was published I knew there was something about writing picture books I had failed to grasp.

Jerry and I both had an interest in the black cowboys of the old West. In *Long Journey Home* I had written a story called "The Man Who Was a Horse," about an actual black cowboy named Bob Lemmons who captured herds of mustang by making the horses believe he was one of them. Jerry liked the story and I rewrote it as the text for a picture book. When Jerry read it he said, "There isn't enough for me to illustrate." I didn't understand.

I happened to have a speaking engagement near his home in Croton-on-Hudson, New York, and drove over early to get together with him. We sat around his dining room table and each of us talked about our creative process. Listening to him I began to understand that in a picture book the illustrations must carry the story so that a child who cannot read can still go through the book and grasp the story. Thus, there has to be a delicate balance between the images created by the illustrator and the images created in the reader's mind by the author's words. By the end of the afternoon Jerry and I were pleased to realize that what each of us cared about most was what was best for the book. If that meant his modifying an illustration or my cutting text so an illustration had more space, we would gladly do it for the good of the book.

Jerry was ready to start working on *Black Cowboy, Wild Horses* when I approached him about doing a new version of *Little Black Sambo*. Phyllis was willing to extend Jerry's deadline for *Black Cowboy, Wild Horses*.

No single story in the English language has been more reviled for its negative stereotyping of blacks than *Little Black Sambo*. If bookstores and libraries even carried it they did not put it on display. I remembered reading the story when I was around seven, and how the big red lips and coal black skin of the characters had made me feel ashamed. Yet, I had never been able to forget the tigers turning to butter and Little Black Sambo eating all those pancakes at the end of the book. I wondered if my own love of pancakes had not stemmed from that last scene.

As I read and reread Helen Bannerman's story I understood that in the dimension of the heart, *Little Black Sambo* was authentic. What child could not relate to a little boy, threatened by physical danger from tigers, who emerges victorious and whole? It was a wonderful story and all it needed was a change of names and new illustrations. (At the time neither Jerry nor I knew that the late Fred Marcellino was doing precisely that in *The Story of Little Babaji,* which would be published at the same time as *Sam and the Tigers.*)

I didn't want to just retell Little Black Sambo. I wanted to take a work that was synonymous with racism and transform it into a black folktale. How to do that? Every time I looked at Bannerman's text I knew I could not improve on her extraordinary economy of language. But in my research I learned that Bannerman had written this story, among many others, to entertain her children while the family was living in India. So she placed her story in Africa but included elements of India with which her children were familiar, namely tigers. One criticism levelled at the story has been that tigers do not exist in Africa. What this criticism misses is that, of course, Bannerman knew there were no tigers in Africa. Her intention was to create a fantasy. I decided to do the same but approach the text midrashically and fill in the gaps in the story. Where did the little boy live? Why did he have new clothes? What kind of place was this that tigers talked to people and people to them?

However, before I could answer those questions I had to do something about the names Bannerman had given the boy and his parents—Black Sambo,

Black Jumbo, and Black Mumbo. I wanted names that would echo the originals in their sense of verbal play, but without, simultaneously, evoking the racist implications they have now.

One morning I awoke thinking about the story. I started saying the name Sam to myself, over and over. Suddenly out of my mouth came, "Sam-sam-sa-mara." I got out of bed and hurried to the computer where I wrote: "Once upon a time there was a place called Sam-sam-sa-mara." And I knew immediately that in Sam-sam-sa-mara everyone was named Sam.

Where Bannerman had told the story with an economy of language I went in the opposite direction and used alliteration and big words—"Mr. Giraffe's Genuine Stupendous Footwear Emporium" and metaphors in which concrete objects were compared to emotions—"a pair of silver shoes shining like promises that are always kept." I created new animal characters and brought in Brer Rabbit and other animal characters from the Uncle Remus tales and created a black coming-of-age story.

Jerry and I had no way of knowing how our version of a hated story would be received. But we were aware that most people under the age of thirty had never heard of *Little Black Sambo*. For them *Sam and the Tigers* was nothing more than a story. However, those who could not divorce themselves from their personal and historical associations with *Little Black Sambo* did not react to *Sam and the Tigers* as if it were merely a story. Some blacks wondered why Jerry and I had wasted our talents resurrecting it. But the late Virginia Hamilton understood when she wrote (*Horn Book,* November–December 2000) that she considered *Sam and the Tigers* to be a "future classic.... I'm eternally grateful ... for *Sam and the Tigers* by Julius Lester, illustrated by Jerry Pinkney. Sam is revolutionary in its re-visioning of *Little Black Sambo.*"

I had certainly been aware that even more than in retelling the Uncle Remus stories I was confronting history in doing a new version of *Little Black Sambo.* It is not enough to be opposed to racism. One must transform the images of blackness as Western history has presented them to us, and this means transforming old stories and creating new ones. These new stories will be rooted in tradition, but so deeply that a listener will be able to hear the steady and rhythmic beating of a heart, his own heart, maybe even every heart. Among the great wonders, the great mysteries, and the great truths of being human is the sound of a heart throbbing from within the dark silence at the center of a story.

North Vietnam, 1967

Change the name and it's about you, that story.

Horace, *Satires,* bk. I, 1.69

Sometimes I wonder if there isn't something a little absurd about being in my mid-sixties and writing for children. What do I know about being a child in this time? Perhaps more than I realize.

On September 11, 2001, the attacks on the World Trade Center in New York, the Pentagon outside Washington, D.C., and the failed attack that resulted in the plane crash in a Pennsylvania field, plunged our individual universes into a chaos beyond anything we could have ever imagined. It is a kind of chaos created when we can no longer assume we are safe in the world, when we find ourselves having to live with an unremitting anxiety that we can die, not because of anything we as individuals have done, but simply because we are. It is a kind of chaos created when we find our lives at the mercy of people who do not know us or care about us. It is the kind of chaos I grew up with in the 1940s and 1950s in the segregated South, the kind of chaos now common to children in Israel, Gaza, the West Bank, Rwanda, Argentina, Brazil, the Congo, to name just a few places.

The psychic chaos created by the events of September 11 had its origins in stories many Muslims in the world have about America and Americans. Just as we consider their stories about us to be untrue, they consider our stories about them in the same way. Stories do not have to be true to be powerful, to be believed, to be acted on. By definition, stories are not beneficent. Stories whites created about blacks circumscribed my childhood like a prison. Stories blacks tell about Jews make me a pariah to some blacks. Stories shape our feelings and actions toward other ethnic and religious groups, races, and individuals.

It is important to take responsibility not only for the stories we tell but, perhaps more, the stories we listen to and believe. Throughout human history it has been all too common for us to believe the worst of others, to even be eager to hear and believe the worst of each other. It is all too common for groups to create a camaraderie of righteousness among themselves by creating stories about another group that casts them as unrighteous. Such spiritual sloth has led to the deaths of untold millions all over the globe.

This laziness is no longer acceptable. We know

better. The promise of story is that it enables us to use our imaginations and take residence in another's skin, to whatever extent that is possible, to whatever extent we can. But using the imagination requires that we must make an effort and all too many do not want to because they do not want to risk discomfort.

I was told by a woman that she'd had to buy a copy of my novel *When Dad Killed Mom* (Harcourt/ Silver Whistle, 2001) for a course she was taking, but the title frightened her and she hadn't read it. I have received similar responses to other books, such as *To Be a Slave* and *From Slave Ship to Freedom Road* (Dial Books, 1998), in which I've asked readers to enter black suffering. Reading about the suffering of others— whether it is two children who must learn how to live after their father murdered their mother or the terror that was slavery and is racism—is negligible compared to the pain of those who live with it.

Education does us a disservice by placing a premium on the faculty of reason. To what extent does reason enhance the quality of our living? To what extent does reason bring the quality of mercy to our living? The failure of modern living is the failure of the imagination, the failure to look at ourselves through the eyes of someone else, the failure to see ourselves as equals in the realm of the soul. Story can enable us to experience other modes of being and recognize who we are and who we might become—if we allow ourselves to be open and vulnerable to the humanity that story, at its best, can offer.

It is summer 1956. I am seventeen years old and that fall I will be entering college. I remember my senior English class and the English poet Percy Bysshe Shelley. Something about him, yes, caught my imagination. I go to the library and check out a biography of Shelley. He had been an atheist and to me, the son of a fundamentalist Methodist minister, the thought that someone in the world had not believed in God was revolutionary. In his atheism Shelley presented me with the possibility that there were other ways to be than the one in which I had been raised.

I can still see the seventeen-year-old me sitting beneath the large tree in our front yard making my first attempts at writing poetry and by the end of that summer I had reached a tentative but daring decision: I thought I wanted to be a writer.

Because of Shelley I reimagined what was possible for my life and responded to something in my soul which had theretofore not been recognized: I didn't have to be a minister like my grandfather and father. I would be a writer even though reason derided and mocked me.

I am convinced that if I can bring you into my being through the use of the imagination, I have created the possibility that you and I will see that we are more alike than we may have thought. Reimagining possibilities presents us with a moral imperative to transcend the narrow collective identities of race, ethnicity, religion, and gender and put on that broadest of collective identities, our finite humanity.

In 1978 the now deceased novelist John Gardner published a small book called *On Moral Fiction*. It was daring of him to use the word *moral*, because he risked guilt-by-association with those who seek to ban books, legislate personal behavior, and have us all re-created in the image of a god who is a perfect reflection of them. But, morality is not a prescription list of do's and don'ts. Morality is about the spirit we bring to our living, and, by implication, to story. If, in the presence of a person or a book, we feel ourselves mysteriously but unmistakably confirmed as human beings, if we sense that life itself is being celebrated in this book or person, then we are in the presence of the moral.

John Gardner put it this way: "We recognize art by its careful, thoroughly honest search for and analysis of values. It is not didactic because, instead of teaching by authority and force, it explores, open-mindedly, to learn what it should teach. It clarifies and confirms . . . [M]oral art tests values and rouses trustworthy feelings about the better and the worse in human action."

Perhaps the key phrases are "thoroughly honest

search" and "explores, open-mindedly." We are not accustomed to conceiving of the moral either as searching or exploring "open-mindedly," or imaginatively. We do not often encounter human beings who search with care and thoroughness for values, who explore with open minds to learn what they should teach (and even when merely walking, we are teaching something about how to be in the world).

Many years ago I had a book of short stories for the adult market rejected by an editor who preferred fiction that put extraordinary people in extraordinary situations because she was curious to see what would happen. My stories put ordinary people in ordinary situations because that is who we are—ordinary people living in ordinary situations of family, school, work, and leisure. This is why much of my work has focused on the lives of the ordinary people who are the bedrock of history. The books about slavery and the books of folkloric retellings are different expressions of the same moral imperative—the communication of the humanity of those whose humanity has been denied, and to be a guide for readers to live, in the imagination, what others lived in the flesh.

Being such a guide imposes on the writer a responsibility to create the language through which we recognize our souls. And perhaps this responsibility weighs more heavily on those of us who write for children. It should because it is through our words that children first encounter the possibilities of language, first understand that there are words for inchoate feelings, and that words can give one the power not only to express what is inside, but through words one gains the power to create feelings and pictures in others.

Writing is a sacred trust in which I reimagine the possibilities of living in the soul for myself as well as others. My books are consciously directed at the soul of the reader, which means that what I write is an expression of my soul, ancestral and/or personal. I define the soul as that piece of the divine put into my keeping, that piece of the divine placed in your keeping.

My sacred trust as a writer embraces all people. This dimension is absent from conventional morality that pits an Us against a Them, that separates people from each other and does not invite us into what Henry James described as life's "buzzing, blooming confusion."

I was initiated into this process of reimagining possibilities in a gift from my first wife. She gave me a human skull, something I had mentioned casually one day that I thought would be interesting to own. Imagine my surprise when she happened to see one in the window of a curio shop in New York's Greenwich Village and bought it for me.

I did not know how to respond when I opened

the gift box to see someone's skull inside. At first I was afraid of it. I felt pity for whoever this had been and I tried to imagine what kind of life one had to have led for his or her head to end up in the window of a shop in Greenwich Village. I put the skull beside my type-writer and over the days and weeks I began to know it. I would stare at the sockets where its eyes had been, the holes of its nostrils, the exposed teeth. I would hold the skull and press the bones beneath the eye sockets and then I would press my face in the same places until I felt the identical spot. Gradually I became aware of the skull beneath my skin.

As I became more acquainted with the skull, I was intrigued by the fact that I had no idea whether this person had been male, female, white, black, Christian, Jewish, or atheist. I knew a physical anthropologist could have told me the person's gender and even have reconstructed his or her face, but I preferred only what I could see with my untrained eye. What I saw was myself.

I began looking at people and seeing the skull beneath the skin. I realized that we are all skulls. A hundred years from now if all our skulls were placed side by side, no one would know which one was me and which was you. Yet, we prize our individuality as if it is the rarest of jewels. We live as if the story of humanity began with our births and will end with our deaths.

Here resides the wonder and the challenge. We are at once unique individuals with special attributes and gifts and we are only skulls. Our years as skulls will be infinitely longer than our few years as unique individuals. A hundred years from now no one will know that most of us were here. We can only hope our names may appear on a line in a genealogical chart in the care of the descendant who is the keeper of Joseph's bones in his generation.

So, when I write, it is my sacred trust to write to your skullness, to love and cherish the fact that we are all skulls and life is all too short and we will all die much too soon. This is the human reality and because this is so, how absurd to invest meaning in nationality, in skin color and whether one has breasts or a penis, and whether one goes to this church or that mosque. How pathetically stupid!

I take seriously the Unseen and the Unknowable, regarding it and living in relationship to it as if it is seen and known. An interviewer once asked the novelist Joyce Carol Oates whom she wrote for. She replied simply, "God." What that means for me is when I write, my audience is that part of you which exists beyond and separate from definitions of gender, race, and all the socio-political definitions which hang from our limbs and rattle like the chains of Jacob Marley's ghost. There is a sacred place in each of us, whether we know it or not. It is from that place I seek to write and it is to that place in you my words seek to go.

But if this relationship I want to participate in with you is to exist, you must take responsibility for that sacred place in yourselves. You must take responsibility for the Unseen and the Unknowable and the mystery of it all—the terror and the awe, and the beauty, because as the German poet Rilke wrote in the first of the *Duino Elegies*—"beauty's nothing/but the start of terror we can hardly bear."

In Judaism we speak of *tikkun haolam,* repair of the universe, meaning that it is the responsibility of each of us to make the universe whole, and the only way to do that is to take responsibility for that portion of the universe put into our keeping, namely, ourselves.

Reb Simcha Bunim, a Hasidic rabbi, wrote:

The Lord created the world in a state of beginning. The universe is always in an uncompleted state, in the form of its beginning. It is not like a vessel at which the master works to finish it; it requires continuous labor and renewal by creative forces. Should these cease for only a second, the universe would return to primeval chaos.

My sacred trust as a writer does not differ one whit from my sacred trust as a human being, does not differ from your sacred trust, namely to live with reverence toward and responsibility for our souls.